Fibonacci Applications and Strategies for Traders

WILEY TRADER'S ADVANTAGE SERIES

John F. Ehlers, *MESA and Trading Market Cycles*
Robert Pardo, *Design, Testing, and Optimization of Trading Systems*
Gary Klopfenstein and Jon Stein, *Trading Currency Cross Rates*
Robert Fischer, *Fibonacci Applications and Strategies for Traders*

Fibonacci Applications and Strategies for Traders

Robert Fischer

Series Editor: Perry J. Kaufman

John Wiley & Sons, Inc.

New York • Chichester • Brisbane • Toronto • Singapore

Copyright © 1993 by John Wiley & Sons, Inc.

Library of Congress Cataloging in Publication Data:

Fischer, Robert, 1941 June 17–
    Fibonacci applications and strategies for traders / by Robert
Fischer.
        p.   cm. — (Wiley trader's library)
    Includes index.
    ISBN 0-471-58520-3
    1. Speculation. 2. Stocks. 3. Commodity exchanges. 4. Fibonacci
numbers.   I. Title.   II. Series
HG6041.F573   1993
332.64—dc20   93-7637

To Jens and Claudius,
who graciously tolerated my absences,
and who were missed over the many years
more than I can ever say.

ACKNOWLEDGMENTS

In 1977 Mr. Joachim Bahr-Vollrath of Germany introduced me to the principles of Elliott and Fibonacci. Without the generous sharing of his knowledge—the foundation for this book, I could never have proceeded. Thank you, Mr. Bahr!

After my 1983 Fibonacci seminars, I was fortunate to meet Homer Russell. Homer did an incredible job creating the software on the logarithmic spiral and time analysis used in this book. Without Homer's programming skills, most of the substantiation of the theory would not have been possible.

Even though the knowledge and the programs have been in place since 1985, it took until 1992 for me to put the loose ends together. It started with a visit to Omega Research, Inc. in Miami. Bill Cruz gave me the necessary support to print most of the charts with TradeStation, one of the leading on-line technical information systems. More importantly, I got to know Samuel Tennis. Sam is a senior software technician with Omega Research. His programming skills made it possible for me to analyze corrections and extensions in a way never before possible. Sam's personal engagement contributed substantially to this book.

My biggest problem was getting mentally organized to write this. My son, Jens, a student at the University of Cologne, Germany, was of invaluable help in getting me started and guiding me through the concepts from one chapter to the next. Working so closely with my son was truly the great reward of this book.

Germany is far away and writing in a second language is anything but easy. Whenever I had a chapter drafted, I gave it to Anne Cavanagh. With her indepth knowledge of the markets and her writing skills, she helped to get this book finished.

Mr. Perry Kaufman and I have come a long way together. We collaborated on my first work in 1979, but this time Perry gave me so much more. It is his flair for the written word that shapes this book—not to mention his patience and continued drive for perfection (which hurt at times, but made me work even harder). Thank you, Perry!

R.F.

PREFACE

This book deals with the most fascinating subject in stock and commodity analysis. It is the integration of Nature's Law (seen as a behavioral phenomenon) into price studies to create a serious and reliable investment tool. New discoveries with the Fibonacci summation series open the window for a price-time analysis that can pinpoint tops and bottoms with a stunning accuracy.

For 50 years, R.N. Elliott has remained a legend for legions of analysts. Without his ideas, this book could never have been written. His brilliant deductions include:

- Market swings are a reflection of human behavior.

- Human behavior can be related to a phenomenon of nature.

- Nature's law can be measured by using the Fibonacci summation series.

From his findings, published in *The Wave Principles*, Elliott claims that he can forecast price movements.

Here we separate ourselves from Elliott. We consider this impossible and will prove it. Because of the wave count, the Elliott concept becomes highly subjective.

Instead, we approach the markets by focusing strictly on the Fibonacci summation series and ignoring the wave count. This removes all subjectivity and replaces the uncertainty with definitive, tested rules. The introduction of entry and exit rules makes disciplined, even automatic trading possible.

The book begins with an indepth study of the Fibonacci summation series, emphasizing the Fibonacci ratio. It is always surprising to learn that major achievements in the fields of natural science, nuclear theory, radio, and television have this ratio in common. The Fibonacci ratio is not just a numbers game but one of the most important mathematical presentations of natural phenomena ever discovered. We apply this ratio as a geometric tool to equity and commodity price swings using techniques never seen before.

The Fibonacci ratio is best used in forecasting correction targets. However, different strategies are presented, including a very short-term approach for those investors who do not want to hold a position longer than one or two days. A computer study was used to confirm the validity of this strategy.

In addition, the Fibonacci ratio is used to analyze price targets on extensions. Extensions happen in run-away markets. An investment entered at the end of the extension is considered the safest strategy in the Elliott concept.

I introduced the idea of time analysis in 1983 at a seminar in Chicago. Nine years later, with the aid of a computer, it is now possible to show that this analysis is a valid investment alternative.

The final chapter introduces the logarithmic spiral, the investment tool that takes a lot of imagination to believe in. Even though we now have a computer program to draw the spirals, it took us many years to understand it and to develop rules that make it easy to use for investment decisions. This spiral is the link between Nature's Law and human behavior, expressed in the price pattern of stocks and commodities. Price patterns don't happen by accident. The logarithmic spiral allows us to analyze market swings both "price and time" with a precision never seen before.

This book is intended to be educational. Within the size limits of this book, the concepts are presented thoroughly with detailed examples. I hope that you find these ideas as exciting, enlightening, and useful as I have.

ROBERT FISCHER

Chicago, Illinois

THE TRADER'S ADVANTAGE SERIES PREFACE

The Trader's Advantage Series is a new concept in publishing for traders and analysts of futures, options, equity, and generally all world economic markets. Books in the series present single ideas with only that background information needed to understand the content. No long introductions, no definitions of the futures contract, clearing house, and order entry. Focused.

The futures and options industry is no longer in its infancy. From its role as an agricultural vehicle it has become the alterego of the most active world markets. The use of EFPs (exchange for physicals) in currency markets makes the selection of physical or futures markets transparent, in the same way the futures markets evolved into the official pricing vehicle for world grain. With a single telephone call, a trader or investment manager can hedge a stock portfolio, set a crossrate, perform a swap, or buy the protection of an inflation index. The classic regimes can no longer be clearly separated.

And this is just the beginning. Automated exchanges are penetrating traditional open outcry markets. Even now, from the time the transaction is completed in the pit, everything else is electronic. "Program trading" is the automated response to the analysis of a computerized ticker tape, and it is just the tip of the inevitable evolutionary process. Soon the executions will be computerized and then we won't be able to call anyone to complain about a fill. Perhaps we won't even have to place an order to get a fill.

Market literature has also evolved. Many of the books written on trading are introductory. Even those intended for more advanced audiences often include a review of contract specifications and market mechanics. There are very few books specifically targeted for the experienced and professional traders and analysts. *The Trader's Advantage Series* changes all that.

This series presents contributions by established professionals and exceptional research analysts. The authors' highly specialized talents have been applied primarily to futures, cash, and equity markets but are often generally applicable to price forecasting. Topics in the series will include trading systems and individual techniques, but all are a necessary part of the development process that is intrinsic to improving price forecasting and trading.

These works are creative, often state-of-the-art. They offer new techniques, in-depth analysis of current trading methods, or innovative and enlightening ways of looking at still unsolved problems. The ideas are explained in a clear, straightforward manner with frequent examples and illustrations. Because they do not contain unnecessary background material they are short and to the point. They require careful reading, study, and consideration. In exchange, they contribute knowledge to help build an unparalleled understanding of all areas of market analysis and forecasting.

I first met Robert Fischer through his manuscript, *Stocks or Options? Programs for Profits* (Wiley, 1980). It has originally been published in German and he was struggling to make the concepts clear to English-speaking readers. I was impressed by his intense desire to communicate that information to others. I helped him with the translation because of my belief that every author wants the quality of his or her publication to be the very best.

Robert has always been fascinated by the patterns that continually appear on price charts. Long before his options book, he had devoured all the information available on Elliott's wave principles. He traded Elliott's method for years, always looking for ways to improve its consistency and remove subjectivity.

When he began to realize the importance of Fibonacci numbers within chart analysis, you could see the electricity in his research. He absorbed the subtleties of Fibonacci ratios, studying plants, architecture, and human behavior. In 1983, I attended the Fibonacci Seminars where Robert introduced the use of *time goal days* as a method of forecasting based on Fibonacci ratios. Everyone was enthralled by the concept that human behavior often favored certain proportions. While most traders now embrace Fibonacci retracement levels of 38 percent, 50 percent, and 62 percent, Robert was still far ahead of them by applying these ratios to forecasting *event days*. He added depth and consistency to chart trading.

But he was still unhappy with the results. I watched Robert search to find a solution that was more accurate and yet consistent with what he believes is the underlying behavioral force in the market. Then he found the logarithmic spiral, one of the most sophisticated phenomenon in nature. Integrated into his analysis, it combines both price and time in a dynamic way.

In the mid-1980s, I was asked to program the formulas so that these logarithmic spirals could appear on a screen along with the price chart. A trader would be able to sit and watch price movement as it reached a support or resistance level indicated by the spiral. Being good at math, I underestimated the difficulties and was soon swimming in pages of formulas. And, this was before I got to the point of deciding whether to rotate the spiral clockwise or counterclockwise.

Fortunately, it was just then that Robert found Homer Russell. I made a graceful exit, but was disappointed that Homer didn't seem to need any of my equations. It wasn't long before the logarithmic spiral program was operational.

In this book, Robert Fischer covers all of the important steps that resulted in combining Elliott and Fibonacci in his unique way, bringing it to the point of its development today. It is filled with new ideas and clear expectations. Until you reach the very end, the techniques require no mathematical skills. After that, a computer program provided in Appendix B will do the rest.

I am very pleased that Robert has been able to write this book. I know of no one with a better understanding of Elliott's method and Fibonacci's principles, and no one who has worked harder to put them together.

PERRY J. KAUFMAN

Vermont
June 1993

CONTENTS

Fibonacci Applications and Strategies for Traders

1

THE FIBONACCI RATIO

THE FIBONACCI SUMMATION SERIES

Let your imagination soar. Think of the universe, the constellations, the galaxy. Contemplate the beauty and form of all the wonders of nature: the trees, the oceans, flowers, plant life, animals, and even the microorganism in the air we breathe. Give further thought to the achievements of man in the fields of natural science, nuclear theory, medicine, radio, and television. It may surprise you to learn that all of these have one thing in common—the *Fibonacci Summation Series.*

In the thirteenth century, Thomas of Aquinas described one of the basic rules of aesthetics—man's senses enjoy objects that are properly proportioned. He referred to the direct relationship between beauty and mathematics, which is often measurable and can be found in nature. Man instinctively reacts positively to clear geometrical forms, in both his natural environment and in objects created by him, such as paintings. Thomas of Aquinas was referring to the same principle that Fibonacci discovered.

Fibonacci, a mathematician, lived in 1175. He was one of the most illustrious scientists of his time. Among his greatest achievements was the introduction of Arabic numerals to supersede the Roman figures. He developed the Fibonacci summation series:

1, 1, 2, 3, 5, 8, 13, 21, 34, 55, 89, 144, . . .

This mathematical series develops when, beginning with 1, 1, the next number is formed from the sum of the previous two numbers. But what makes this series so important?

The series tends asymptotically (approaching slower and slower) toward a constant ratio. However, this ratio is irrational, that is, it has a never-ending, unpredictable sequence of decimal values stringing after it. It can never be expressed exactly. If each number in the series is divided by its preceding value (e.g., 13 ÷ 8), the result is a ratio that oscillates around the irrational 1.61803398875 . . . , being higher one time and lower the next. But never in eternity can the precise ratio be known to the last digit. For the sake of brevity, we will refer to it as *1.618*.

This ratio had begun to gather special names even before Luca Pacioli (a medieval mathematician) named it the *Divine Proportion*. Among its current day names are the *Golden Section*, the *Golden Mean*, and the *Ratio of Whirling Squares*. Kepler called the ratio "one of the jewels in geometry." Algebraically it is generally designated by the Greek letter phi ($\Phi = 1.618$).

The asymptotic tendency of the series, its ratio's ever-tightening oscillation around the irrational phi, can be best understood by showing the ratios of the first few entries in the series. This example takes the ratio of the second entry to the first, the third to the second, the forth to the third, and so forth:

$1:1 = 1.0000$, which is lower than phi by 0.6180
$2:1 = 2.0000$, which is higher than phi by 0.3820
$3:2 = 1.5000$, which is lower than phi by 0.1180
$5:3 = 1.6667$, which is higher than phi by 0.0486
$8:5 = 1.6000$, which is lower than phi by 0.0180

As we continue in the Fibonacci summation series, each member will divide into the next one by a closer and closer approximation of phi which *can never be reached*.

We will see later that the individual numbers in the Fibonacci summation series can be seen in commodity price movements. The swings of the ratios around the value 1.618 by either higher or lower numbers will be found in the *Elliot Wave Principle* described as the *Rule of Alternation*. Man subconsciously seeks the Divine Proportion; it satisfies his comfort level.

Dividing any number of the Fibonacci sequence by the following number in the series asymptotically approaches the ratio 0.618, which is simply the reciprocal of 1.618 (1 ÷ 1.618). But this is also a very unusual, even remarkable phenomenon. Since the original ratio has no end, this ratio must also have no end.

Another important fact is that the square of any Fibonacci number is equal to the number in the series before it, multiplied by the number after it, plus or minus 1.

$$5^2 = (3 \times 8) + 1$$
$$8^2 = (5 \times 13) - 1$$
$$13^2 = (8 \times 21) + 1$$

Plus and minus continually alternate. Again this phenomenon is an implicit part of the Elliott Wave Principle called the *Rule of Alternation*. It states that complex corrective waves alternate with simple ones, strong impulse waves with weak impulse waves, and so on.

THE DIVINE PROPORTION IN NATURE

It is remarkable how many constant values can be calculated using the Fibonacci sequence, and how the separate figures of the sequence recur in so many variations. However, it cannot be stressed too strongly that this is not just a numbers game but *the most important mathematical presentation of natural phenomena ever discovered*. The following illustrations depict some interesting applications of this mathematical sequence.

The Pyramid of Gizeh

Many people have tried to penetrate the secrets of the Pyramid of Gizeh. It is different from the other Egyptian pyramids because it is not a tomb, but rather an unsolvable puzzle of figure combinations. The marvelous ingenuity, skill, time, and labor used by the designers of the pyramid to erect a perpetual symbol demonstrates the supreme importance of the message they desired to convey to posterity. That era was preliterary and prehieroglyphic and symbols were the only means of recording inventions.

The key to the geometrical and mathematical secret of the Pyramid of Gizeh, so long a puzzle to mankind, was actually handed to Herodotus by the temple priests when they informed him that the pyramid was designed in such way that the area of each of its faces was equal to the square of its height (Figure 1–1).

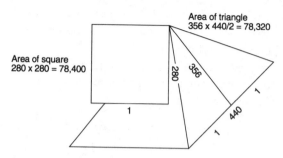

Figure 1-1   Structure of Pyramid of Gizeh.

One edge of the Pyramid of Gizeh is 783.3 feet long, the height of the Pyramid is 484.4 feet. The length of one sideline divided by height leads to the phi ratio 1.618. The height of 484.4 feet corresponds to 5,813 inches (5-8-13)—figures from the Fibonacci sequence. These interesting observations give a clue that the pyramid was designed to incorporate the phi proportion 1.618. Modern scientists tend towards the interpretation that the ancient Egyptians built it for the sole purpose of transmitting knowledge they wanted to preserve for coming generations. Intensive research at the Pyramid of Gizeh has shown how far advanced mathematical and astrological knowledge was at that time. With respect to all proportions in and around the pyramid, the number 1.618 played the most important role.

The Mexican Pyramids

Not only are the Egyptian pyramids built according to the perfect proportions of the Golden Section, but the same phenomenon is found in the Mexican pyramids. It is conceivable that both the Egyptian and the Mexican pyramids were built at approximately the same time by people of common descent. Figures 1-2a and b give an example of the importance of the incorporated proportion, phi = 1.618.

A cross-section of the pyramid (Figure 1-2a) shows a structure shaped as a staircase. There are 16 steps in the first set, 42 in the second, and 68 in the third. These numbers are based on the Fibonacci ratio 1.618 in the following way:

$$16 \times 1.618 = 26$$
$$16 + 26 = 42$$
$$26 \times 1.618 = 42$$
$$42 \times 1.618 = 68$$

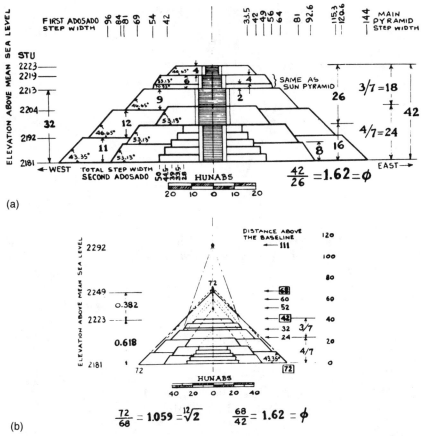

(a)

(b)

Figure 1–2 Number phi = 1.618 incorporated in the Mexican pyramid. (*Source: Mysteries of the Mexican Pyramids,* by Peter Thomkins (New York: Harper & Row, 1976) p. 246, 247. Reprinted with permission.)

The Plants

A different representation of Fibonacci numbers is found in the number of axils on the stem of a plant as it develops. An ideal case can be seen in the stems and flowers of *sneezewort* (Figure 1–3). A new branch springs from the axil and more branches grow from the new branch. When the old and new branches are added together, a Fibonacci number is found in each horizontal plane.

The golden numbers come into view again if we examine the occurrence of petals of certain common flowers. For example:

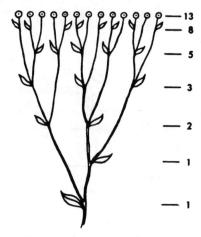

Figure 1–3 Fibonacci numbers found in the flowers of sneezewort. (*Source: The Divine Proportion,* by H.E. Huntley (New York: Dover, 1970) p. 163. Reprinted with permission.)

Iris	3 petals
Primrose	5 petals
Ragwort	13 petals
Daisy	34 petals
Michalmas Daisy	55 and 89 petals

The number and arrangement of the florets in the head of a member of the composite family is a particularly beautiful example of golden numbers found in nature.

We were looking for laws that worked in the past and therefore have the highest probability of continuing to work in the future. In the Fibonacci ratio, we seem to have found such a law.

THE FIBONACCI RATIO IN GEOMETRY

The existence of the Fibonacci ratio in geometry is well known, but applying this ratio as a geometric tool to commodity prices with spirals and ellipses has never been done before. The reason is that it is necessary to use the power of computers to apply the logarithmic spiral and logarithmic ellipse as an analytic tool.

Both the spiral and ellipse have unusual properties consistent with the Fibonacci ratio in two dimensions, price and time. It is very likely that the integration of spirals and ellipses will elevate the interpretation and use of the Fibonacci ratio to another, much higher level. Up to now the Fibonacci ratio was used for measurement of corrections and extensions of price swings. The time element forecast was seldom integrated because it did not seem to be as reliable as the price analysis. By including spirals and ellipses in a geometric analysis, both price and time analysis can be combined accurately.

The Golden Section of a Line

The Greek mathematician Euclid related the Golden Section to a straight line (Figure 1–4). The line AB of length L is divided into two segments by point C. Let the length of AC and CB be a and b, respectively. If C is a point such that $L:a$ equals $a:b$, then C is the *Golden Section AB*. The ratio $L:a$ or $a:b$ is called the "Golden ratio." In other words, the point C divides the line AB into two parts in such a way that the ratios of those parts is 1.618 and .618.

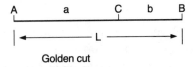

Golden cut

Figure 1–4   Golden section of a line.

The Golden Section of a Rectangle

In the Great Pyramid, the rectangular floor of the King's chamber illustrates the Golden Section (Figure 1–5). A "Golden Rectangle" can best be demonstrated by starting with a square—the basic area of the Pyramid of Gizeh. Side AB of the square $ABCD$ in Figure 1–5 is bisected. With the center E and radius EC, an arc of a circle is drawn cutting the extension of AB at F. Line FG is drawn perpendicular to AF, meeting the extension of DC at G. Then $AFGD$ is the Golden Rectangle. According to the definition, the Golden Section Rectangle is 1.618 times longer than it is wide. The ratio of its proportions is therefore phi:

$$1.618:1$$

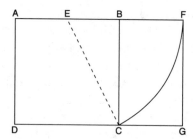

Figure 1–5   Golden section of a rectangle.

Greek architects and sculptors incorporated this ratio into their work. Phidias, a famous Greek sculptor, made use of it; the proportions of the Parthenon at Athens illustrate this. Built in the fifth century B.C., it is based on a triangular pediment, which is still intact. Its dimensions exactly fit into the Golden Rectangle. It stands as an example of the aesthetic value of this unique shape.

The Logarithmic Spiral

The only mathematical curve to follow the pattern of growth is the *logarithmic spiral,* expressed in the spira mirabilis or the nautilus shell (Figure 1–6). The logarithmic spiral is called the most beautiful of mathematical curves. This spiral has been a common occurrence in the natural world for millions of years. The Golden Section and the Fibonacci series are all associated with this remarkable curve.

Figure 1–6 shows a radiograph of the shell of the chambered nautilus (nautilus pompilius). The successive chambers of the nautilus are built on the framework of a logarithmic spiral. As the shell grows, the size of the chambers increases, but their shape remains unaltered.

We will demonstrate the geometry of the logarithmic spiral using the Golden Rectangle *ABCD* (Figure 1–7) with *AB* : *BC* = phi : *1.* Through point *E,* called the "Golden Cut" of *AB,* line *EF* is drawn perpendicular to *AB* cutting the square *AEFD* from the rectangle. The remaining rectangle *EBCF* is a Golden Rectangle. If the square *EBGH* is lopped off, the remaining figure *HGCF* is also a Golden Rectangle. Assume that this process is repeated indefinitely until the limiting rectangle *O* is so small that it is indistinguishable from a point.

Figure 1–6   Logarithmic spiral. (*Source: The Divine Proportion,* by H.E. Huntley (New York: Dover, 1970) p. iv. Reprinted with permission.)

The limiting point O is called the *pole of the equal angle spiral,* which passes through the Golden Cuts D, E, G, J . . . (the sides of the rectangle are nearly, but not completely, tangential to the curve).

The relation of the Fibonacci series is evident from Figure 1–7, for the spiral passes diagonally through opposite corners of successive squares, such as $DE, EG, GJ,$ . . . . The lengths of the sides of these squares form a Fibonacci series. If the smallest square has a side of length d, the adjacent square must also have a side of length d. The

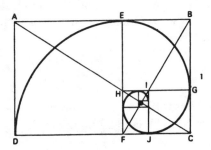

Figure 1–7   Geometry of the logarithmic spiral. (*Source: The Divine Proportion,* by H.E. Huntley (New York: Dover, 1970) p. 101. Reprinted with permission.)

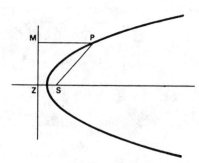

Figure 1–8 Logarithmic ellipse. (*Source: The Divine Proportion,* by H.E. Huntley (New York: Dover, 1970) p. 71. Reprinted with permission.)

next square has a side of length *2d* (twice as long), the next of *3d,* and so on, forming the series *1d, 1d, 2d, 3d, 5d, 8d, 13d,* . . . which is exactly the Fibonacci Series *1, 1, 2, 3, 5, 8, 13,* . . . .

Two segments of the spiral may be different in size, but they are not different in shape. The spiral is without a terminal point; while growing outwards (or inwards) indefinitely, its shape remains unchanged. The logarithmic spiral is the link between the Fibonacci Summation Series and the World of Nature.

The Logarithmic Ellipse

Important curves are found in nature. The most significant to civilization include the horizon of the ocean, the meteor track, the parabola of a waterfall, the arcs traced in the sky by the sun and the crescent moon, and the flight of a bird.

An *ellipse* is the mathematical term for an oval. Each ellipse can be precisely designated by only a few characteristics. The extreme form of an ellipse is the parabola (Figure 1–8), which can be represented mathematically as:

$$y^2 = 4ax$$

Point *P* is equidistant from a fixed point *F* (the focus) and a fixed line *ZM* (the directrix). The curve is symmetrical about the axis.

2

THE ELLIOTT WAVE
PRINCIPLE IN A NUTSHELL

Ralph Nelson Elliott was an engineer. After a serious illness in the early 1930s, he turned to the analysis of stock prices, especially the Dow Jones Index. After a number of remarkably successful forecasts, Elliott published a series of articles in *Financial World Magazine* in 1939. In these, he first presented his contention that the Dow Jones Index moves in rhythms. According to Elliott, everything moves with the same pattern as the tides—low tide follows high tide, reaction follows action. Time does not affect this scheme, because the structure of the market in its entirety remains constant.

In this chapter we will review and analyze the following concepts of Elliott:

- Nature's Law
- The "Secret of the Universe"
- The Wave Principle
- Interpretative market letters.

The focus of this section will be on the main areas of Elliott's work that have long-lasting value. Even if we do not agree with some of Elliott's findings, he must be admired for his ideas. We know how difficult it is to create a new concept without the technical support we have available today. When we began to study Elliott's work in 1977, it was a tremendous struggle to get the data needed for an indepth analysis. How much more difficult must it have been for Elliott when he started his work! With the computer technology available today, we have the ability to test and analyze quickly, but it is still necessary to have Elliott's ideas in order to begin.

Elliott wrote, "Nature's Law embraces the most important of all elements, timing. Nature's Law is not a system, or method of playing the market, but it is a phenomenon which appears to mark the progress of all human activities. Its application to forecasting is revolutionary."*

Elliott based his discoveries on Nature's Law. He notes, "This law behind the market can only be discovered when the market is viewed in its proper light and then is analyzed from this approach. Simply put, the stock market is a creation of man and therefore reflects human idiosyncrasy" (Elliott, p. 40).

This chance to forecast price moves motivates legions of analysts to work day and night. We will focus on the ability to forecast, and try to answer whether or not it is possible.

Elliott was very specific when he introduced his concept. He said, "All human activities have three distinctive features, pattern, time and ratio, all of which observe the Fibonacci summation series" (Elliott, p. 48).

Once the waves can be interpreted, the knowledge may be applied to any movement as the same rules apply to the price of stocks, bonds, grains, cotton, and coffee. The most important of the three factors is pattern. A pattern is always in progress, forming over and over. Usually, but not invariably, you can visualize in advance the type of pattern. Elliott describes this market cycle as, ". . . divided primarily into 'Bull Market' and 'Bear Market'" (Elliott, p. 48). Figure 2–1 subdivides the bull market into five "major waves" and the bear market into three major waves. The major waves 1, 3, and 5 of the bull market as subdivided into five "intermediate waves" each. Then each of the intermediate waves 1, 3, and 5 subdivides into five "minor waves."

*The Complete Writings of R.N. Elliott with Practical Application from J.R. Hill, J.R. Hill, Commodity Research Institute, N. Carolina, 1979 (subsequent references will cite Elliott), p. 84.

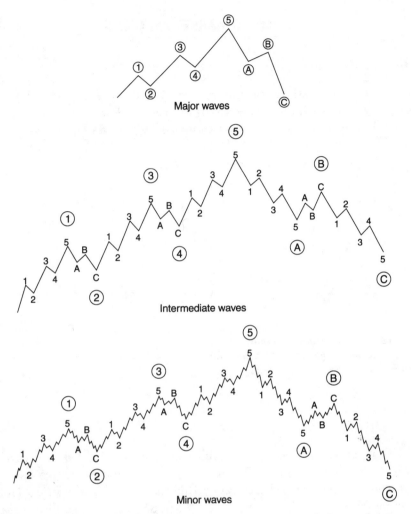

Figure 2–1 Elliott subdivided the "perfect" stock market cycle into major, intermediate, and minor waves.

The problem with this general market concept is that, most of the time, there are no regular 5-wave swings. More often, the 5-wave swing is the exception. To fine tune the concept, Elliott introduced a series of market patterns which take care of almost every situation. The most important ones are described next.

ELLIOTT'S MARKET PATTERNS

The 5-Wave Swing

If the market rhythm is regular, wave 2 will not retrace to the beginning of wave 1, and wave 4 will not correct lower than the top of wave 1. If it does, the wave count must be adjusted (Figure 2–2).

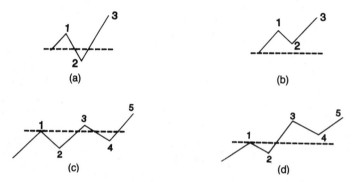

Figure 2–2   (a) Erroneous counting in a 5-wave up-swing; (b) correct counting in a 3-wave up-swing; (c) erroneous counting in a 5-wave up-swing; (d) correct counting in a 5-wave up-swing.

Corrections

Each of the corrective waves 2 and 4, can be subdivided into three waves of a smaller degree. The correction wave 2 and corrective wave 4 alternate in pattern. Elliott called this the *rule of alternation*. This means that, if wave 2 is simple, wave 4 will be complex, and vice versa. This is shown in Figure 2–3.

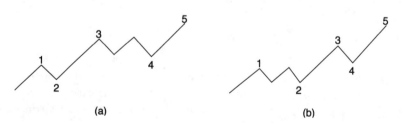

Figure 2–3   (a) Wave 2 is simple; wave 4 is complex; (b) wave 2 is complex; wave 4 is simple.

With this remarkable observation, Elliott linked Nature's Law with human behavior. In the sunflower, pinecone, or pineapple there are spirals that alternate by first turning clockwise and then counter-clockwise. This alternation repeats itself in the corrective wave 2 and wave 4.

There are three types of corrections:

1. Zigzag in a downtrend (the opposite for the uptrend).

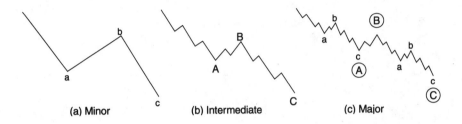

(a) Minor   (b) Intermediate   (c) Major

2. Flats in a downtrend (the opposite for the uptrend).

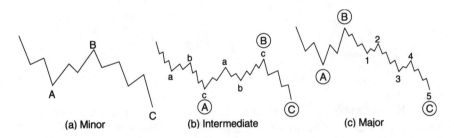

(a) Minor   (b) Intermediate   (c) Major

3. Triangles in an uptrend or downtrend.

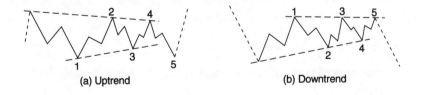

(a) Uptrend   (b) Downtrend

"The student cannot be certain that a triangle is forming until the fifth wave has started," observed Elliott (p. 53). This makes it very difficult to forecast price moves.

Elliott noticed that the standard type of corrections were not enough to cover all market actions. Therefore he added the complex corrections, which he describes as:

1. Minor correction of three waves

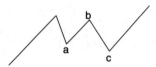

2. Double sideways correction with seven waves

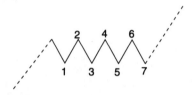

3. Triple sideways corrections with seven waves.

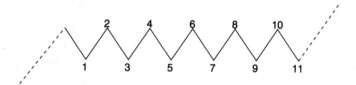

Elliott made the statement, "It is possible however to know when elongated wave c will occur by understanding the rule of alternation" (p. 51). It is not clear that it is possible to forecast wave c; and if it were, it is not obvious that this rule is of any value for the investor. The corrections are so complex that it is impossible to determine, in advance, any of the following essential points:

• The length of wave c

• The current state of the correction (i.e., is this a simple, double or triple formation)

• What wave will come next.

Elliott never indicated either a definitive entry or exit rule to use when trading. This means that the trader must use subjectivity and initiative to implement Elliott's ideas.

Extensions

"Extensions may appear in any one of the 3 impulse waves wave 1, 3, or 5 but never in more than one" (Elliott, p. 55). Figures 2–4 and 2–5 show extension for uptrends and downtrends, respectively.

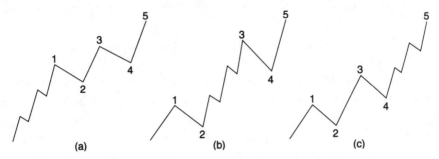

Figure 2–4 (a) First wave extension in uptrend; (b) third wave extension in uptrend; (c) fifth wave extension in uptrend.

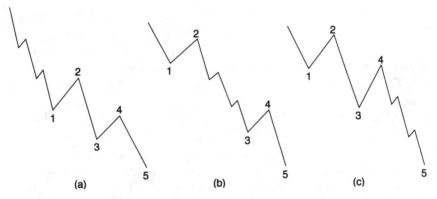

Figure 2–5 (a) First wave extension in downtrend; (b) third wave extension in downtrend; (c) fifth wave extension in downtrend.

"It will be noted that in each instance there are a total of 9 waves, counting the extended wave as 5 instead of 1. On rare occasions an extended movement will be composed of 9 waves, all of equal size" (Elliott, p. 55). For example, Figure 2–6 shows an uptrend and downtrend, each consisting of nine waves.

According to Elliott, extensions have the following characteristics:

• They occur only in new territory of the current cycle; they do not occur in corrections.

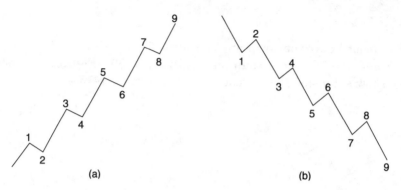

Figure 2–6 (a) 9-wave extension in uptrend; (b) 9-wave extension in downtrend.

- They are doubly retraced, that is, a correction will pass over the same ground twice, down and up.

- If extensions occur in wave 3, double retracement will be satisfied by wave 4 and wave 5.

All of the possibilities that Elliott introduced and described in his publications have not been shown here. The purpose of this review was to show the essence of Elliott's ideas and follow them as they become more intricate. In its most complex stages, it is even difficult for an experienced Elliott follower to apply these rules to real-time trading.

Elliott admitted, "Corrections in bull and bear swings are more difficult to learn" (p. 48). The problem seems to be that the complex nature of the wave structure does not leave room to forecast future price moves in advance. It looks perfect in retrospect. The multitude of rules and situations described by Elliott can be used to fit any price pattern after the fact. But that is not enough.

FIBONACCI RATIO

Elliott is given the most credit for introducing the Fibonacci summation series as an investment tool. He wrote, "Later I found that the basis of my discoveries was a law of Nature known to the designers of the Great Pyramid 'Gizeh' which may have been constructed 5000 years ago. Fibonacci visited Egypt and on his return disclosed a Summation Series" (Elliott, p. 42). Chapter 1 presented the series:

1, 1, 2, 3, 5, 8, 13, 21, 34, 55, 89, 144 . . .

Dividing any number of the Fibonacci sequence by the next higher number in the series causes the series to converge asymptotically to the ratio:

$$1.618 \ (1:1.618 = 0.618)$$

Elliott recognized the importance for this summation series and he wrote, "From experience I have learned that 144 is the highest number of practical value. In a complete cycle of the stockmarket, the number of minor waves is 144." The breakdown of this complete cycle is shown in the Table 2–1.

The entire Fibonacci summation series is employed here. Elliott stated, "The length of waves may vary, but not the number of waves. The numbers of this series are useful in timing the waves, both advancing and declining" (pp. 45, 129).

The general application of this principle is that a move in a particular direction should continue until such time that it completes a number consistent with the Fibonacci summation series. This phenomenon is best illustrated in Figure 2–7.

A move that extends itself beyond 3 days should not reverse until 5 days are reached. A move that exceeds 5 days should last 8 days. A trend of 9 days should not finish before 13 days, and so on. This basic structure of calculating trend changes applies equally for hourly, daily, weekly and monthly data. But this is only an "ideal model," and one must never expect commodity prices to behave in such a precise and predictable manner. Elliott noted in his *Nature's Law* that deviations can occur in both *time* and *amplitude,* and individual waves are not likely to always develop in this regular pattern.

Table 2–1

Number of	Bull Market	Bear Market	Total
Major waves	5	3	8 complete waves
Intermediate waves	21	13	34 complete waves
Minor waves	89	55	144 complete waves

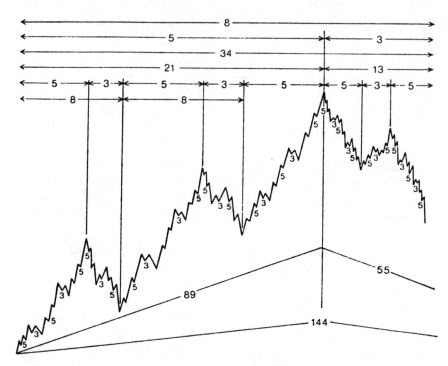

Figure 2–7 Fibonacci Summation Series integrated into the complete cycle of the stock market from Elliott.

TREND CHANNELS

To make his analysis more definitive, Elliott tried to solve the timing problem with trend channels, parallel lines drawn across the bottom and top of a price move. The trend channels are used only to forecast the end of wave 5.

In an upwards movement of five waves, a base line is drawn across the bottom (the end) of waves 2 and 4. Then a parallel line is drawn through the highest point wave 3 (Figure 2–8).

Elliott noted, "Usually wave 5 will end approximately at the parallel line, when [an] arithmetic scale is used. However, if wave 5 exceeds the parallel line considerably and the composition of wave 5 indicates that it has not completed its pattern, then the entire movement, from the beginning of wave 1, should be graphed on semi-log scale. The end of wave 5 may reach, but not exceed, the parallel line" (p. 60). If the same figures were graphed on both scales, the pictures would appear as in Figure 2–9.

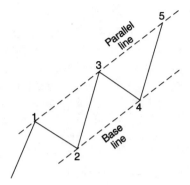

Figure 2-8 Trend channel to forecast the end of wave 5.

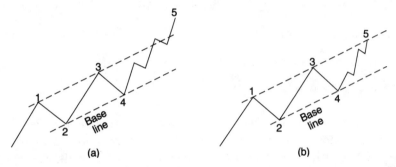

(a)   (b)

Figure 2-9 (a) Wave 5 exceeds the parallel line of trend channel on arithmetic scale; (b) wave 5 touches parallel line of trend channel when graphed on semi-log scale.

SUMMARY

The Elliott Wave principles are brilliantly conceived. They work perfectly in "regular" markets and give stunning results when looking back at the charts. The most significant problem is that market swings are irregular. This makes it difficult to give definitive answers to questions such as:

• Are we in an impulse wave or corrective wave?

• Will there be a fifth wave?

• Is the correction flat or zigzag?

• Will there be an extension in wave 1, 3, or 5 ?

Elliott said, "The Principle has been carefully tested and used successfully by subscribers in forecasting market movements" (p. 107). In another place he mentioned, "Hereafter letters will be issued on completion of a wave and not await the entire cycle. In this matter, students may learn how to do their own forecasting and at no expense. The phenomenon and its practical application become increasingly interesting because the market continually unfolds new examples to which may be applied unchanging rules" (p. 137).

My own work with the Elliott concept, from many different angles over 15 years, does not support the contention that the wave structure has forecasting ability. The wave structure is too complex, especially in the corrective waves. The rule of alternation is extremely helpful, but this does not tell us, for example, whether to expect:

- A correction of 3 waves.

- A double sideways correction.

- A triple sideways movement.

It is even more unlikely that any 5-wave pattern can be forecast. The integration of extensions in wave 1, wave 3, or wave 5 complicates the problem even more. The beauty of working with the Elliott concept is not the wave count. We can only agree when J. R. Hill writes in his practical applications, "The concept presented are extremely useful but have literally driven men 'up the wall' as they try to fit chart patterns to exactness in conformity with the Elliott wave" (Elliott, p. 33).

Elliott is focused on pattern recognition. His whole work is streamlined to forecast future price moves based on existing patterns. He does not appear to have succeeded in this area. Elliott expressed uncertainty about his wave count himself when he wrote in different newsletters, "The five weeks sideways movement was devoid of pattern [—] a feature never before noted" (Elliott, p. 167). "The pattern of the movement across the bottom is so exceedingly rare that no mention thereof appears in the Treatise. The details baffle any count" (p. 165). "The time element [Fibonacci sequence] as an independent device, however, continues to be baffling when attempts are made to apply any known rule of sequence to trend duration" (p. 180). "The time element is based on the Fibonacci Summation Series but has its limitations and can be used only as an adjunct of The Wave Principle" (Elliott, p. 186).

Elliott did not realize that it is not the wave count that is important, but the Fibonacci ratio. It is the Fibonacci ratio that represents

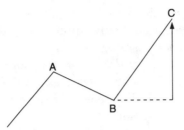

Figure 2–10   Forecasting price move from point B to point C not possible.

Nature's law and human behavior. This is what we try to measure in the market swings. While the Fibonacci ratio is constant, the wave count is confusing.

By studying Elliott's publications carefully, a rule with forecasting value can be identified as "A cyclical pattern or measurement of mass psychology is 5 waves upward and 3 waves downward, total 8 waves. These patterns have forecasting value—when 5 waves upward have been completed, 3 waves down will follow, and vice versa" (Elliott, p. 112).

We could not agree more with this statement. Most likely, Elliott did not realize that his strategy had taken a complete shift. Elliott tries to forecast a price move from point B to point C based on market patterns. We consider this impossible, and Elliott has never given a rule that showed that he was able to do this mechanically (Figure 2–10).

Elliott's latest statement takes exactly the opposite strategy. Instead of forecasting a price move from point B to point C, he waits to the end of a 5-wave move, because 3 waves in the opposite direction can be expected (Figure 2–11).

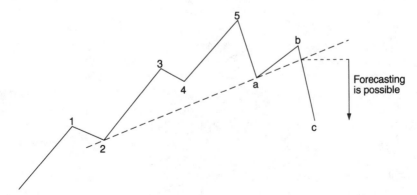

Figure 2–11   Forecasting price move after the end of a 5-wave cycle possible.

We totally agree with Elliott's approach here and will complement the idea with additional rules in later sections. We will also introduce other investment strategies closely related to the Fibonacci ratio. Elliott never worked with a geometric approach. We will introduce *logarithmic spirals* as an investment tool. We strongly believe that this is the solution to the problem of combining 'price and time.' This has never been done before.

The concentration will be on Fibonacci. The following chapters will work with daily and weekly data. Research shows that intraday data can be applied where only daily data has been used thus far. More historical tests are needed before definitive rules can be set.

3

WORKING WITH A
5-WAVE PATTERN

Returning to Elliott's original work, one of his most important statements is, "A cyclical pattern or measurement of mass psychology is 5 waves upward and 3 waves downward, total[ing] 8 waves. These patterns have forecasting value—when 5 waves upward have been completed, 3 waves down will follow and vice versa" (p. 112). This appears to be the only time that Elliott gave a definitive rule with forecasting value, and many times the market behaves exactly as this pattern dictates.

In this chapter, we will analyze this great observation of Elliott, combining it with additional rules to give definitive entry and exit points. Consistent with the Elliott concept, the end of the fifth wave is considered to be a safe point to invest. The rare case of an "extension in the 5th wave" will be explained later.

The five waves can be seen in charts of any time period, whether intraday, daily, weekly, or monthly. The greatest problem for the investor is waiting for the end of the fifth wave. To identify the five-wave swing, we must return to Elliott who said:

- Under normal circumstances, wave 5 appears similar to wave 1.

- Most of the time, wave 3 is the longest wave.

- Wave 4 should not touch the top of wave 1 in an uptrend.

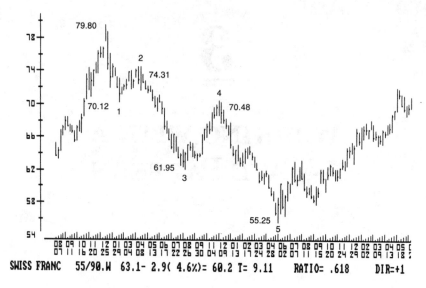

Figure 3–1   5-wave swing on weekly Swiss franc chart from 07-07-89 to 06-30-92. (*Source:* TradeStation, Omega Research, Inc.)

Following this path, the weekly chart of the Swiss franc was chosen to demonstrate a 5-wave swing (Figure 3–1).

In Figure 3–1, the 5-wave swing is comprised of:

- Wave 1 from 79.80 to 70.12

- Wave 2 from 70.12 to 74.31

- Wave 3 from 74.31 to 61.95

- Wave 4 from 61.95 to 70.48

- Wave 5 from 70.48 to 55.25

PREDICTING THE END OF
WAVE 5 USING A TREND CHANNEL

Elliott tried to forecast the end of wave 5 by working with trend channels. In an upward movement of five waves, a base line is drawn across the ends (lowest prices) of wave 2 and wave 4. A parallel line is then

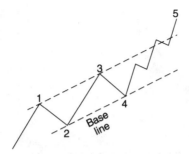

Figure 3–2   Upper line of the trend channel is penetrated.

drawn across the highest point of wave 3 (Figure 3–2). When the five waves are complete, there are a number of options for entering the market. The following cases show the different possibilities for investing at the time wave 5 ends.

Case 1

"Usually wave 5 will end approximately at the parallel line, when an arithmetic scale is used" (Elliott, p. 60).

If a trade is entered when the upper line of the trend channel is touched, it runs the risk of the market going even higher. Elliott never gave a solution for protecting an investment against the risk of a wrong analysis.

Case 2

"If wave 5 exceeds the parallel line considerably and the composition of wave 5 indicates that it has not completed its pattern, then the entire movement, from the beginning of wave 1, should be graphed on a semi-log scale. The end of wave 5 may reach, but not exceed the parallel line" (Elliott, p. 60).

If the market price reaches the trend channel of a semi-log chart (Figure 3–3a), it is positioned at a very good point to invest, but only when combined with the conservative entry and exit rules introduced later. The only problem is that this situation is very rare and not likely to be reached. Waiting until the price touches the upper trend line runs the risk of missing the move entirely (Figure 3–3b).

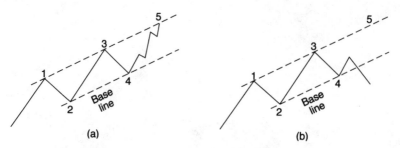

Figure 3–3 (a) Trendline on semi-log chart is touched; (b) trendline on semi-log chart is not touched.

Case 3

"When 5 waves upward have been completed, 3 waves down will follow." (Elliott, p. 112). Using this approach, we would:

- Wait for 5 waves to be completed.
- Wait for the a,b correction.
- Invest when wave c penetrates the base line.

This strategy is shown in Figure 3–4. This is a very conservative approach, and the pattern can be found over and over again in the charts. The advantage of this strategy is that:

- The market has already changed trend direction at the time of entry, and
- There is still good profit potential, measured by the combined amplitude of all five waves. (For example, Figure 3–5 shows how powerful this signal can be in the Japanese yen.)

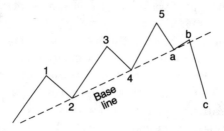

Figure 3–4   Complete cycle of 5 impulse waves and 3 corrective waves.

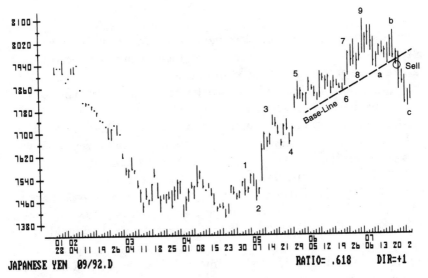

Figure 3–5   Daily chart Japanese yen from 01-01-92 to 07-25-92. Sell signal at an a-b-c correction. (*Source:* TradeStation, Omega Research, Inc.)

The disadvantage of this strategy is that:

- The trading opportunity can be missed if there is no *a-b-c* correction, and
- It is valid only for major moves. Smaller swings can often have corrections that are too small to be profitable.

PREDICTING THE END OF
WAVE 5 WITH FIBONACCI RATIOS

The end of wave 5 may also be identified by integrating the Fibonacci ratios into the analysis. We have already learned that there are two ratios in the Fibonacci Summation Series, 1.618 and 0.618, that can be used.

By integrating the Fibonacci ratios into the 5-wave pattern, shown in the weekly chart of the Swiss franc (see Figure 3–8), *price goals* can be calculated. But even before that can be done, the *swing size* must be defined.

Swing Size

A price *swing* is continuous movement in one direction. Because prices often move up and down in very small increments, it is necessary to ignore some of this "noise" by eliminating all movement that does not continue in one direction for at least a minimum point value. If, on successive days, the Swiss franc were to move +50, +100, −30, −10, +70, −20, +25, and the minimum swing size was 50 points, we would only see an upwards move of 185. The 40 and 20 point reversals were less than the 50-point filter; therefore, they are ignored.

A minimum swing size is needed to make the best use of the Fibonacci ratios. For that reason, intraday charts and examples are not used in this book. Shorter time intervals contain more "noise," that is, price movement that is random and therefore not predictable. In addition, the magnitude of that noise is relatively large compared to the swing size possible during a short interval. The inclusion of more noise would obscure the useful information and make analysis ineffective.

Elliott noted, "In fast markets, the daily range is essential, and the hourly useful, if not always essential. On the contrary, when the daily range becomes obscure, due to slow speed and long duration of waves, condensation into weekly range clarifies" (p. 139).

The intent of this book is not to present empirical tests for every commodity, but to present a concept with adequate convincing data. As a guideline for examples, the minimum swing size for a daily chart of the Swiss franc, Deutsche mark, or Japanese yen will be 100 basis points. For the British pound, it will be 200 basis points. When using weekly charts, the swing size will be twice the size of that used on the daily chart.

Confirmation of the Swing Highs and Lows

A swing high or low is confirmed when there is a counterswing of at least the minimum swing size in the opposite direction. For example, the minimum swing size is 100 basis points, prices must decline by at least 100 points (without being interrupted by a net upwards move of 100 points) to confirm a swing high. This is shown in Figure 3–6.

Minimum Amplitude of the Total Five Swings

Elliott noted that after a 5-wave swing pattern there will be a 3-swing correction. But this approach only makes sense if the amplitude of the 5-swing pattern is reasonably big. Even though Elliott noted, "Timing

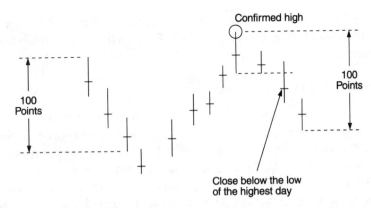

Figure 3–6 Confirmation of a swing high.

is the most essential element. What to buy is important, but when to buy is more important," (p. 84) he never gave a clear rule for entering and even more important, for liquidating a position.

Consider a perfect 5-wave count within a 200 basis point up-swing. It would be unrealistic to expect a profit from a short position following the strategy described in case 3.

The reason for this is as follows: The minimum correction allow-able using the Elliott concept is 38% (the transformed Fibonacci ratio 0.618) of the total amplitude of a 5-wave cycle.

This strategy leaves only a small profit margin for a move of 200 basis points. Yet it is a perfect strategy—one of the best in all of Elliott's work. If we have a larger amplitude of 1,000 basis points,

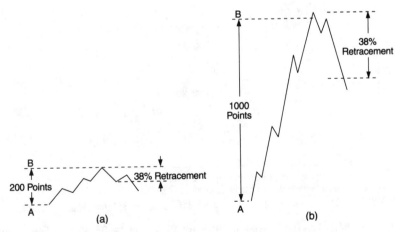

Figure 3–7 (a) 200-point swing with 38% retracement; (b) 1000-point swing with 38% retracement.

waiting for the end of wave 5 and selling into the *a-b-c* correction is a very interesting strategy (Figure 3–7). This pattern can be seen in the markets over and over again.

Wave 1 and the Fibonacci Ratio 1.618

Elliott never gave definitive rules to apply his concept to the markets. We will try to introduce rules that make the Elliott concept safer to trade. The weekly Swiss franc (Figure 3–8) will be used as an example of how the Fibonacci ratio can be used with wave 1.

Whenever there is a 3-swing pattern, the extreme point of wave 5 can be calculated using the Fibonacci ratio 1.618 (Figure 3–9). It is not possible to know whether this extreme point will ever be reached, but we do know that this precalculated price level is very important should the prices reach this level. The following shows how to calculate the end of wave 5 using the ratio 1.618 applied to the weekly Swiss franc chart (Figure 3–8):

Start of wave 1	79.20	9.08×1.618	$= 14.69$
Bottom of wave 1	70.12	$70.12 - 14.69$	$= 55.43$ price
Difference	9.08 points		target

Then, the real time bottom of wave 5 was 55.25.

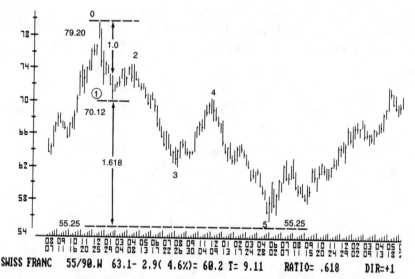

Figure 3–8 Weekly chart Swiss franc from 07-07-89 to 06-30-92. The ratio 1.618 is used with wave 1 to calculate the end of wave 5. (*Source:* TradeStation, Omega Research, Inc.)

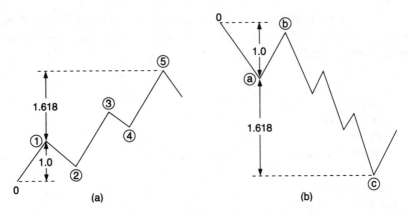

Figure 3–9 (a) The ratio 1.618 is used with wave 1 to calculate the end of wave 5; (b) the ratio 1.618 is used with wave a to calculate the end of wave c in a correction.

THE AMPLITUDE OF WAVES 1, 2, AND 3, AND THE FIBONACCI RATIO 0.618

Whenever the peak of wave 3 is established, the end of wave 5 can be precalculated using the ratio 0.618 (Figure 3–10). How do we know that the peak of wave 3 is established?

- Wave 3 must to be longer than wave 1, and
- In an uptrend, wave 4 should not go lower than the bottom of wave 2 (the opposite for a downtrend) (Figure 3–10).

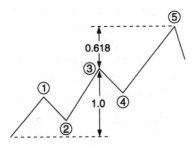

Figure 3–10 The total amplitude of the wave 1, 2, 3, is used with the ratio 0.618 to calculate the end of wave 5.

By analyzing the weekly Swiss franc chart, the end of wave 5 can be calculated based on the total amplitude of the first three waves multiplied by 0.618 as follows:

Start of wave 1	79.20
Bottom of wave 3	61.95
Difference	17.26 points
17.26 × 0.618 =	10.66
61.96 − 10.66 =	51.29 price target

Two price targets can then calculated for end of wave 5, using the two ratios 1.618 and 0.618:

Amplitude of wave 1 × 1.618 =	55.25 (see p. 32)
Amplitude of all 3 waves × 0.618 =	51.29

Do we know whether the forecasted price level will ever be reached? Absolutely not. We can never know in advance whether these levels will be reached. But should these levels ever be reached, there is an excellent chance of a trend change.

It is better when the precalculated price targets are close. But in reality this happens very rarely. Most of the time there is a price target band—the difference between the two targets (55.25 and 51.29)—as seen in Figure 3–8. Whenever this price band exists, the trader must decide where and when to enter the market.

The entry rule must be integrated into the analysis. To complete the strategy, a stop-loss rule must also be introduced, as well as a re-entry rule, profit target and trailing stops. Each of these steps will be described in detail.

Entry Rule. Whenever a 5-wave swing has been identified, a confirmation of the trend change must occur before entering the market. The following two situations are possible:

1. After waiting for the precalculated price targets to be reached, the market reverses a little too early and the trade is missed. We do not want "chase" the price.

2. After waiting patiently, the buy order gets filled in the falling market. Instead of reversing exactly at the precalculated price, the market keeps falling.

These dilemmas can never be totally solved, but our experience tells us that the effect can be smoothed by working with an entry rule. The trade-off in working with an entry rule is that part of the move which we want to capture must be sacrificed. But it has the advantage of not entering the market too early and not suffering losses that result from an extension in wave 5. (This case will also be discussed in more detail later.)

The entry rule is based on the findings of Elliott, which indicate that, after every 5-wave pattern, there is an *a-b-c* correction, or a double retracement. Once wave *a* and wave *b* are completed, we can sell into wave *c* if the previous valley is broken (Figure 3–11). The opposite is true for a buy signal.)

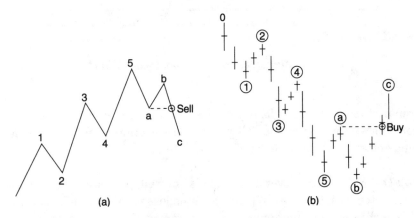

Figure 3–11   (a) After the end of a 5-wave pattern, we can sell into wave c; (b) after the end of a 5-wave pattern, we can buy into wave c.

This is a very conservative approach. In our opinion, it is one of the most important of Elliott's discoveries. This pattern can be found on the daily chart of the Japanese yen (Figure 3–12) as it develops.

The approach is conservative because it has the disadvantage that the trend change might be completely missed if there is no *a-b-c* correction, but a strong trend reversal instead. More aggressive investors who want to buy may do better entering an order in advance of the point where the close is higher than the high of the low day (and the opposite for a sell signal), as shown in Figure 3–13.

Again, this is a more aggressive approach. It runs the risk of getting stopped out when there is a wave 5 extension. A trader must be

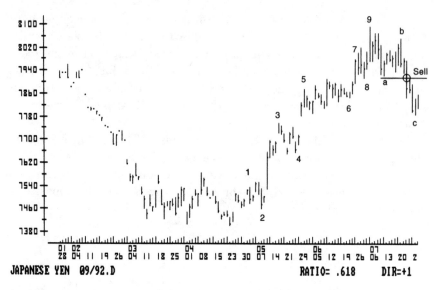

Figure 3–12 Sell signal after an a-b-c correction. (*Source:* TradeStation, Omega Research, Inc.)

prepared for a string of losing trades when a double or triple correction follows the end of the 5th wave. The selection of entry rules depends on the risk preference of the investor.

Stop-Loss Rule. Whenever a position is entered, it should be protected with a stop loss. One way of placing a stop loss is to use a *price square*. This technique can be applied to all commodities, all charts, and is easy to use.

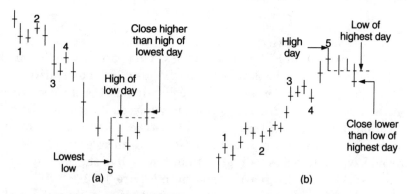

Figure 3–13 (a) Buy signal when the close is higher than the high of the lowest day; (b) sell signal when the close is lower than the low of the highest day.

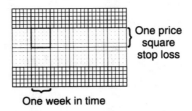

One price
square
stop loss

One week in time

Figure 3–14   Stop loss a "square" above/below the entry point.

To create a price square, measure the distance of five business days (for a daily chart) or five weeks (on a weekly chart). Apply this distance "in time" to the price scale, that is, take the horizontal time measurement and use the same distance vertically for a price stop loss. This gives the stop loss in points on every chart (Figure 3–14). Because the same measurement is used for both horizontal and vertical, the result is considered a "square." Place the stop loss (the price square):

• Above the high of the highest day prior to the short signal, or

• Below the low of the lowest prior to the long signal.

The market must close above/below the square to be stopped out. There are times when the result of this stop-loss rule is a price that is too far from the entry point for a trader, who would rather get stopped out more frequently with small losses than take fewer large losses. One solution is to place the stop loss one tick above/below the previous peak/valley after entering the market (Figure 3–15).

Neither of the stop-loss selections is better or worse than the other. It is the risk preference of the individual investor which determines which stop is better one. The most important strategy is to be consistent. Once a strategy is chosen by some tested method, stick with it.

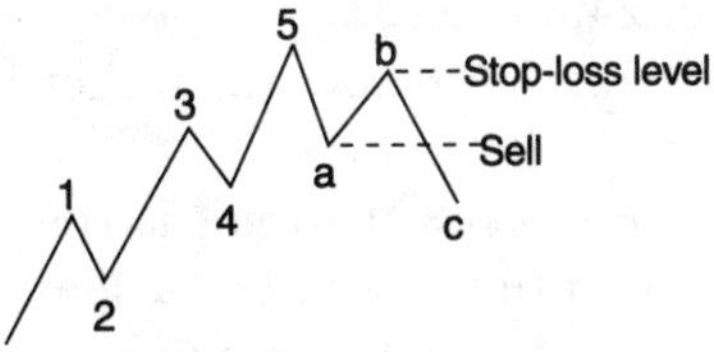

5
b
3
- - -Stop-loss level
a
-Sell
1
4
c
2

Figure 3–15   Stop loss above the previous peak.

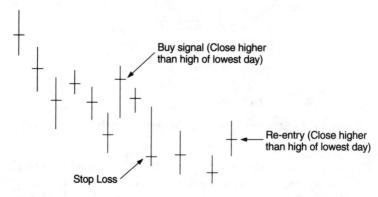

Figure 3–16 **Re-enter after stop loss when close is again higher than high of lowest day.**

Re-Entry Rule. Whenever a position is stopped out, it is re-entered using the following rule (shown in Figure 3–16). This re-entry rule is the same as already described for the entry rule. After a short position is stopped out, it may be re-entered on the short side when the close is lower than the low of the highest day (the opposite for a long position).

Profit-Target Rule. When either a long or short position is held, it can be liquidated at a *profit target* whenever that precalculated value is reached. Using the Swiss franc weekly chart (Figure 3–8) as an example, the profit target is calculated as follows:

1. On Figure 3–8, the weekly Swiss franc chart, the 5-wave swing starts at 79.80, with the low of the 5-wave swing at 55.25.

2. Using a profit target of 38% (the complement of the Fibonacci ratio .618), the calculation is as follows:

$$79.80 - 55.25 = 24.55$$
$$38\% \text{ of } 24.55 = 9.32$$
$$55.25 + 9.32 = 64.57, \text{ the target price}$$

For a long position, the profit target is the 38% retracement of the distance from the high to the low. For a short position, the profit target would be a 38% retracement from the low to the high. This case is shown in Figure 3–17.

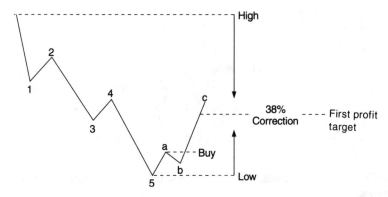

Figure 3–17   The profit target is 38% the distance between high and low.

A correction of 38% is the minimum that can be expected after a completed 5-wave swing. Most of the time, a 50% correction is more likely.

Trailing Stops.   The rule most important to successful commodity trading is "Never give back all of your profits." How many times has it happened that a comfortable profit in a position is lost in a single "blow out," and ends up in a loss? To protect these profits, and as an alternative or addition to the profit target, a *trailing stop* can be used. This strategy has the advantages that:

• Most of the profits that develop can be protected, and

• We can still participate in a trending market.

Of course, the position might get stopped out before the profit target is reached. The decision to use profit targets, the defensive strategy of a trailing stop, or a combination of the two, is an issue of the individual investor's risk preference.

A trailing stop of four days (Figure 3–18), protects the position and offers a good chance of capturing a market trend.

An alternative to a trailing stop (in this example, a long position is held) is to place the stop loss below the previous valley (Figure 3–19). Whenever there is a new, higher valley, the stop is raised. In a trending market, the position might be held for a long time.

There is no "best" stop-loss rule. Both of these have their advantages and disadvantages. It is most important that stops are used to protect profits and reduce risk.

Figure 3–18 Four-day trailing stop offers a good chance of capturing part of a market trend.

Figure 3–19 Trailing stop on previous valley.

INVESTING WITH OPTIONS

Options can easily be used as an alternative strategy to futures, but only if the "right" strike price and expiration month are chosen. One problem with options is that the options premium always works against the buyer. As the selected expiration is farther out, the premium increases due to the "time value."

Without going into too much detail, the following ideas might improve trading performance by using options instead of futures:

• When working within a price band, only buy an option when the second price band is reached (Figure 3–20).

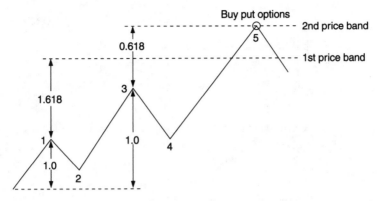

Figure 3–20   Buy of put options when the 2nd price band is reached.

- If the second price band is not reached, wait for wave *a* and wave *b* to be completed, then invest in wave *c* following the entry rule. That is, buy or sell when the previous four highs/lows are broken in wave *c* (Figure 3–21).

The advantage of working with precalculated price targets is that we can buy a call into a falling market or buy a put into a rising market. This reduces the premium of the call or the put substantially. An entry rule is not needed to reduce the risk of the position. Figure 3–22 shows the application of an entry signal with a call option futures position.

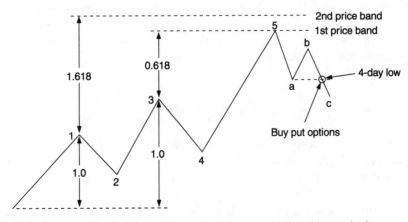

Figure 3–21   Buy of put options when the 1st price band is reached.

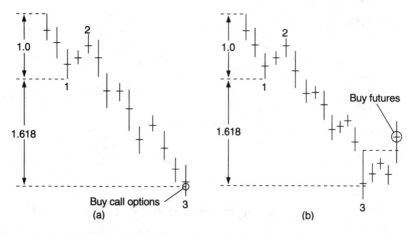

Figure 3–22 (a) The ratio 1.618 is used to calculate the end of wave 3. Buy call options when the target price is penetrated; (b) the ratio 1.618 is used to calculate the end of wave 3. Buy futures when the close is higher than the high of the lowest day.

Buying a call option eliminates the risk of getting stopped out. To be sure that the option moves in tandem with the futures price, always buy the call with a strike price *at* the money or *in* the money. The expiration should be about three months away from the time of entry. If the expiration month is too far away, the option might not run dollar for dollar with the futures price. If the expiration month is too close, the option might expire before the trade is completed.

Options should be substituted for futures only after big price swings. In the Swiss franc, Deutsche mark, or Japanese yen this should be about 10 full points (50.00 to 60.00) measured from the highest high to the lowest low in the 5-wave swing. A big retracement can only be expected in conjunction with a larger.

SUMMARY

The Elliott concept is most famous for the definition of the 5-wave pattern. In a "regular" market, it works with stunning accuracy, but this is not reality. Most of the time there are only "irregular" market patterns.

We consider it impossible to predict or forecast the beginning or end of a 5-wave pattern. But there are very good chances to profit by waiting until a 5-wave pattern has developed. We agree with Elliott when he said, "A cyclical pattern or measurement of mass psychology is 5 waves upward and 3 waves downward, total 8 waves. These patterns have forecasting value; when 5 waves upward have been completed, 3 waves down will follow, and vice versa" (p. 112). But the problem and risk in this strategy is of an extension in the fifth wave, if there was no extension in wave 1 or wave 3 (extensions will be discussed later).

Elliott acknowledged some problems in his concept when he wrote, "Exhaustive research of all available records does not disclose any similar abnormalities to those of the past six months, such as:

- Omission of an intermediate wave (wave 5 of the late bear market),

- Two extensions in one intermediate, or

- Distortion of patterns of the averages" (p. 171).

Elliott must be admired for the tremendous effort to implement his concept with the limited historical data and tools available at that time. But we can not agree with his vision to predict future price moves in general. There are some special rules that can be filtered out. These rules by themselves will give Elliott a place with the great analysts of our century.

The combination of weekly and daily data can improve the quality of the analysis. In order to reduce risk, guidelines were introduced in the situation where wave 5 ends at a point corresponding to the calculation of the Fibonacci ratios 1.618 and 0.618. These guidelines included entry rules to determine entry timing. But entering the market is only part of the investment strategy. We also introduced:

- Stop-loss rules to limit risk.

- Profit targets.

- Trailing stops to capture trend profits.

We have seen that a 5-wave pattern with small amplitude has a small profit potential in the correction. The bigger 5-wave swings have substantial profit opportunity, but occur rarely.

The risk preference of the investor is the most important factor in selecting trading rules.

Options on futures are a very good alternative to outright futures positions when price swings are big; their use takes most of the pressure off finding the perfect entry point. Using an option, we can buy or sell against the market trend, keep the premiums low and have a limited risk. The option should have a strike price *at* or *in* the money, and an expiration date of at least three full months.

4

WORKING WITH CORRECTIONS

According to Elliott, every market moves in rhythms. Impulse waves, defining the major price movement, will have a corrective wave before the next impulse wave reaches new territory. Elliott stated, "Corrections in both bull and bear markets swings are more difficult to learn" (p. 48). Before beginning the analysis of corrections, let us briefly review what has been covered in detail in the previous chapters.

Elliott identified three types of corrections:

1. Zigzags,

2. Flats, and

3. Triangles.

In addition to these, there are the complex corrections:

4. Double sideways corrections with 7 sideways waves, and

5. Triple sideways corrections with 11 sideways waves.

Even though Elliott made the statement, "It is possible however to know when an elongated wave c will occur by understanding the rule of alternation" (p. 51), it does not seem likely that the analysis of corrections have forecasting value. It might be possible to see wave c develop based on the rule of alternation, but this fails to tell us:

- Whether we are in a single, double, or triple correction,

- How far wave c will go, or

- When to enter and exit the position.

On the bottom line, the Elliott concept must make money; it is not just a pleasant mental game. Unfortunately, Elliott does not give the definitive rules for corrections that would allow a trader to reach this goal. The complexity of the corrections leave too much room for subjective decisions.

Used here, *forecasting* does not mean a small breakout of a chart pattern, but the ability to predict a significant price move or change of direction.

Elliott appears to have gotten caught in the complexity of his own concept. The more he noticed the exceptions and tried to integrate them into his concept, the further he moved away from definitive rules.

RULES THAT ARE RELIABLE

There are two definitive rules in the Elliott concept that are reliable:

1. Wave 3 is normally the longest wave.

2. In any impulse or corrective market cycle, we have at least 3 waves.

But these rules get buried in the wave patterns. They are not as challenging as forecasting a price move from point A to point B, but they seem to be extremely reliable and can be applied to any kind of market and commodity.

Following the idealized Elliott concept, the breakdown of a primary market cycle is shown in Figure 4–1, and expressed as:

- Waves 1, 3, 5, a, and c can be subdivided into 5 waves of lesser degree.

- Waves 2, 4, and b can be subdivided into 3 waves of lesser degree.

Figure 4–1 Breakdown of a primary market cycle in the idealized Elliott concept.

Elliott's two great discoveries were expressed when he said, "As will have been noted, all corrective movements regardless of degree are composed of 3 waves," and "It is important to note that wave 3 is never shorter than both wave 1 and wave 5." (pp. 56, 57). From these statements we can draw the conclusion that a future price move can be forecasted if:

- We only concentrate on a 3-wave swing,

- Invest only into the correction of wave 2, and

- Take profits on precalculated price targets.

In this sense, "forecasting" means the ability to identify, in advance, a price move that should allow profits to be taken at a precalculated profit target following specific rules (to be provided later in this chapter).

Figure 4–2 shows profitable areas of investment marked *P1, P2, P3, P4, P5, P6, P7,* and *P8*.

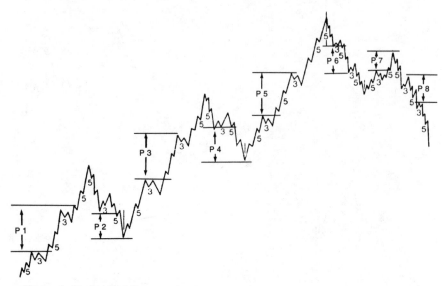

Figure 4–2   Profitable areas for investment based on the Elliott concept.

A 3-wave swing can be expected, most often when the market changes trend direction. There should be good profit potential if:

- Wave 1 has achieved the minimum swing size.
- Wave 3 is longer than wave 1.
- We invest in the correction of wave 2.
- We work with a profit target.
- We always protect our position with a stop loss set at the beginning of wave 1.

This strategy seeks only safe profits from a very special subset of all the market patterns available. It is drawn from the part of the Elliott concept which offers forecasting possibilities within its original rules. But our choice of forecasting is completely different from Elliott's. We have concentrated on a very special combination of events, while Elliott claims to forecast all 5-wave moves. There is no indication that Elliott's method can be successful.

It should be noted that the minimum swing size is a constraint on this strategy, but a necessary one. Without a minimum swing size, the profit potential of many trades will be too small and the result would be frequent whipsaws.

There is also a *maximum swing size*. If there is an initial wave 1 (for example, 2,000 basis points on the British pound weekly chart), it is highly unlikely that either a correction or wave 3 will develop within a reasonable period of time. Elliott said, "On a weekly range chart, all waves of the cycle are clear except those of wave #1, the subdivisions of which are clear in the daily chart. In fast markets the daily range is essential. On the contrary when the daily range becomes obscure, due to slow speed and long duration of waves, condensations into weekly clarifies" (p. 139).

There is no indication that all waves will be clear on a weekly chart. Experience does not confirm this. The problem with big swings in weekly charts, especially in the currencies, is that there are upper and lower bands in which the currencies normally move relative to each other. The Deutsche mark will not move 50 pfennigs against the dollar, even if a 5-wave count predicts it.

WHEN NOT TO INVEST

Following the Elliott concept, we would not buy in an uptrend at the end of wave 3. In Figure 4–3a this point is marked *A,* and in Figure 4–3b it is marked *B.* The reason is that the Elliott concept cannot resolve the dilemma of whether:

- A correction is only part of a long-term trend, or

- A correction is the beginning of a new trend in the opposite direction.

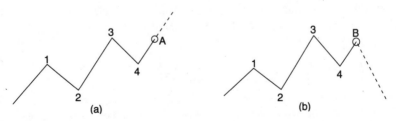

Figure 4–3   (a) No buy at the end of wave 3; (b) no buy at point B.

Figure 4–4   Areas of uncertainty out of the Elliott concept.

Note that the most critical point is at the end of wave 3. Will the final wave 5 develop at point *A* in Figure 4–3a, or is it the beginning of a bigger correction wave as shown in point *B* of Figure 4–3b? Elliott followers might argue that a more detailed wave count or the integration of weekly, daily, and intraday charts might help here. It is not likely, for the complexity of the wave count leaves too much room for error.

In the idealized chart of the Elliott concept shown in Figure 4–4, areas were marked as *X1, X2, X3, X4, X5*. Arguments in favor of Elliott's theory are based on this idealized chart shown in Figure 4–4, but in reality, these chart patterns very rarely occur. Reality is Figure 4–5, a plot of the Dow Jones Industrials between 1960 and 1980. This represents a typical sideways market and can be seen in its many variations on intraday, daily, and weekly versions. Applying the Dow Jones pattern to the mechanical rules of the Elliott concept seems to be impossible.

SIZE OF CORRECTIONS

The most common approach to working with corrections relates the size of the correction to a percentage of the prior move. This approach

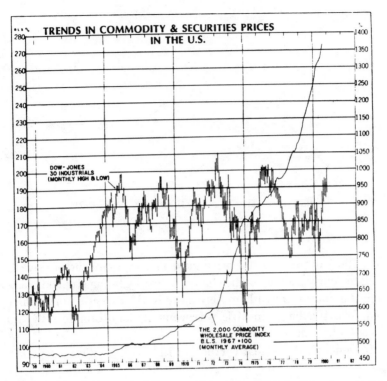

Figure 4–5 Dow Jones 30 Industrials (monthly high-low). (*Source:* Commodity Research Bureau, New York.)

lends itself to the use of the principle ratios of the Fibonacci summation series (Figure 4–6) 0.618, 1.0, and 1.618 from which the three important percentage values are derived:

38% is the result of the division 0.618/1.618.

50% is the transformed ratio 1.000.

62% is the result of the direct ratio 1.0/1.618.

In general, it can be said that, if a 3-swing move is expected, the bigger corrections are better for investing. As the correction gets bigger, so does the profit potential resulting from profit targets (Figure 4–7).

The problem with this approach is that the size of the correction cannot be forecast. A correction can be a retracement of 38%, 50%, 62%,

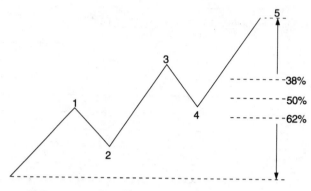

Figure 4–6   Size of corrections 38%, 50%, 62%.

or even 100% of the original price move at the beginning of wave 1. Investing too early increases the chance of loss by being stopped out, even though the market may ultimately move in the direction originally expected. Waiting for a specific retracement, for example 62%, might cause the whole move to be missed.

In general, the safest correction in which to invest depends on:

- The investment strategy (e.g., buy and hold or short-term trading).

- The volatility of the commodity.

- The size of the swing upon which the retracement is measured.

- The strength of the trend.

- The type of data used (i.e., monthly, weekly, daily, or intraday).

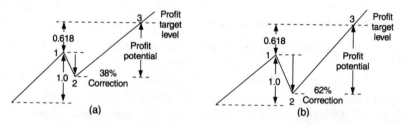

Figure 4–7   (a) Profit potential after 38% correction; (b) profit potential after 62% correction.

CORRECTIONS IN A LONG-TERM TREND

It is generally accepted that trading the correction to a price move can reduce risk. This strategy became very popular in the 1980s for buying securities. By betting on a long-term uptrend, it was easy to buy into the corrections of the Dow Jones or S&P 500. They could always be expected to make new highs, as seen in Figure 4–8. There are many success stories.

Problems with this strategy start when there is no long-term uptrend. Looking at the Dow Jones over the longer period from 1970 to 1980, the pattern of price movement is much more sideways. There were a large number of big swings ranging from about 500 and 1,000 points (Figure 4–9). It is inevitable that patterns such as these will continually reappear.

Figure 4–8 Monthly Dow Jones 30 Industrials Chart from 1982 to 1992. (*Source:* Commodity Quote Graphics, 1992.)

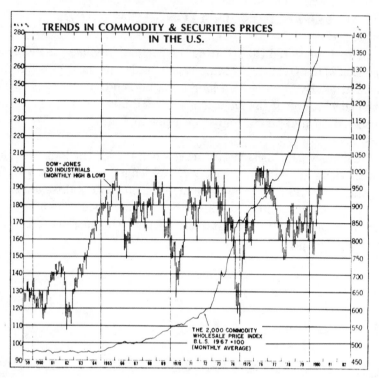

Figure 4–9 Dow Jones 30 Industrials (monthly high-low). (*Source:* Commodity Research Bureau, New York.)

CORRECTIONS IN A SHORT-TERM TREND

Swing Breakout Strategy

In order to show why working with corrections can improve an investment, a simple swing breakout system will be used as an example. Even though this strategy appears to have nothing to do with Elliott or Fibonacci, there is an underlying 3-wave concept that can be closely related to parts of Elliott's theory.

In a simple swing breakout system, a buy entry point occurs at a previous swing high and a sell occurs at the previous swing low. This concept works beautifully as long as there are "regular" markets with big swings, as shown in Figure 4–10. This method does not work well during sideways markets, shown in Figure 4–11.

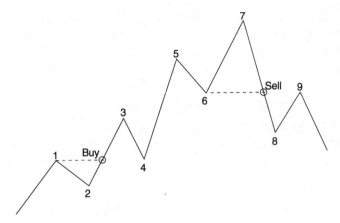

Figure 4–10   Swing breakout system in a trending market.

In order to apply this method, parameters and rules must be fully defined. Different swing sizes, stops, profit targets, trailing stops and re-entry rules can change the performance profile. Different rules also apply when using intraday, daily, or weekly data.

Swing Size.   A swing high on the daily British pound chart is confirmed after a decline of 400 basis points occurs (exceeding the minimum swing value in this example); a low is confirmed after a subsequent rally of 400 points.

Entry Point.   A breakout above the previous swing high is a buy signal; a fall below the previous swing low is a sell signal.

Profit Target.   A profit target established as the total amplitude of swing 1 (the size of the previous swing in the entry direction) times

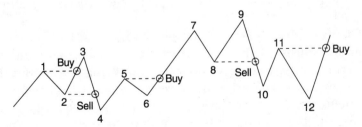

Figure 4–11   Swing breakout system in a sidewards market.

.618 (Figure 4–12). Once this profit target is reached, the current position is exited and no position is entered until the next new entry signal.

Using a hypothetical example (Figure 4–12), the profit target is calculated as:

The total amplitude of wave 1 is	$57.20 - 50.10 = 7.10$
The profit target is 0.618 times the size of wave 1, or	$.618 \times 7.10 = 4.38$
Then, the profit target is	$57.20 + 4.30 = 61.68$

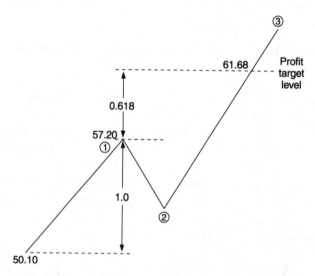

Figure 4–12   The ratio 0.618 is used to calculate the profit target based on wave 1.

Figure 4–13 shows the strategy applied to the daily British pound over a six-month period.

If the price reaches the profit target 61.68, the long position is liquidated.

The strategy of working with a profit target has both advantages and disadvantages. If there is a 3-swing move followed by a trend change, this strategy performs perfectly, capturing profits. But there are two negatives: The price might miss the profit level completely, or we might take profits on the long position only to see the price move much higher. It again depends on the investor's risk preference in making the choice of which strategy to use.

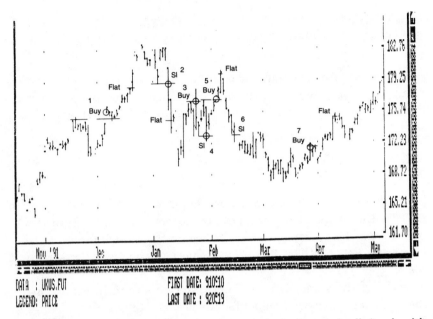

Figure 4–13 Daily British pound from 10-91 to 05-92. Buy and sell signals with profit targets on a swing breakout strategy. (*Source:* System Writer Plus, Omega Research, Inc.)

Stop Loss. For a long position, the stop loss should be chosen as the previous 2-day low and used as a trailing stop (use the opposite for a sell signal).

Trading Signals. The British pound example is intended to demonstrate a very simple swing breakout strategy. It is not intended to be offered as an overall profitable, complete trading system, but as a philosophical approach to how to improve investment strategies related to the Elliott concept. It is based on a swing system, because that is an often-used strategy with its roots in the Elliott concept. With that in mind, the following trade detail shows the hypothetical returns for this method (neither commissions nor slippage have been included):

Trade #1	buy 175.40	sell 182.38	+6.98	
Trade #2	sell 178.90	buy 176.10	+2.78	
Trade #3	buy 176.80	sell 173.12		−3.68
Trade #4	sell 173.10	buy 175.98		−2.88
Trade #5	buy 177.10	sell 179.57	+2.47	

| Trade #6 | sell 172.50 | buy 169.16 | +3.34 |
| Trade #7 | buy 172.06 | sell 174.98 | +2.92 |

The performance profile shows that, as long as there is a trending market, this strategy makes money. But in a sideways pattern such as in January and February 1992, seen in Figure 4–13, the strategy has a string of losing trades.

3-Swing Pattern

In another strategy based on a 3-swing pattern, it is not necessary to wait for the breakout but rather enter directly at the beginning of a correction. The reason goes back to one of the most interesting findings from Elliott, "The 3rd wave is most of the time the strongest wave."

Using the same British pound interval shown in Figure 4–13, the following rules are applied for the new strategy.

Swing Size.   As in earlier examples, there is a minimum swing size. This prevents entering trades that have small profit potential, hence may result in frequent whipsaws. There is also a maximum swing size which limits the magnitude of wave 1 to 2,000 basis points for the British pound. When a swing exceeds the maximum size it is unlikely that a correction will occur, nor should wave 3 develop within a reasonable time.

Corrections.   When working with corrections, it is necessary to choose between:

- Waiting for a 62% correction and run the risk of missing the price move, or
- Investing early and increasing the risk of getting stopped out or having a greater equity drawdown.

If the trader chooses to get into the market, then the entry must be at the time of the correction. The best way to implement this is to combine *swing size, correction,* and an *entry rule.* Table 4–1 refers

Table 4-1   Swing Size, Correction, and Entry Rule

Swing in Points	Correction in %	Entry Rule Previous High/Low
100–200	62	3–4 days
200–400	38	3–4 days
200–400	50	2 days
200–400	62	1 day
400–800	38	3 days
400–800	50	1 day
400–800	62	1 day

to the daily British pound chart shown in Figure 4–13. Other relationships can be established for any commodity.

These are rough estimates resulting from trading experience. For the Swiss franc, Deutsche mark, and Japanese yen, the following swing sizes are used:

Small	50–150	basis points
Medium	150–300	basis points
Large	300–600	basis points

The values for the corrections and for the entry rules are the same as for the British pound. Different products might have different combinations. It is most important to understand that there is a close relationship between *swing size, correction,* and *entry rule.*

Although Elliott never drew this conclusion, it is an improvement which is easily adapted to the Elliott concept, especially because it does not require a wave count.

Entry Rule.   The investment strategy can be fine-tuned by integrating the entry rule. Buying at the beginning of wave 3 is an entry into a falling market. It would be best if the entry rules provided a confirmation of a trend reversal. We can assume that the bigger the swing size and the bigger the correction, the stronger the thrust. Therefore more sensitive entry rules can be defined. These are shown in Figure 4–14. More detailed examples are given in Table 4–1.

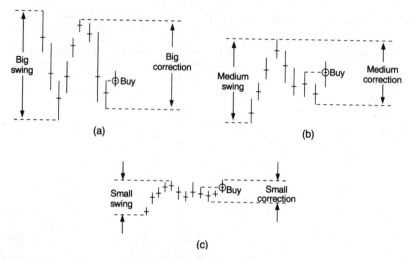

(a)

(b)

(c)

Figure 4–14   (a) Big swing, big correction, previous high entry; (b) medium swing, medium correction, previous two high entries; (c) small swing, small correction, previous three high entries.

In the 1983 seminars on Fibonacci given by the author, a slightly different entry rule was introduced. At that time, a buy signal required that today's close be higher than the high of the lowest day (the opposite for a sell signal). This can be seen in Figure 4–15.

It cannot be said that one entry rule is better than the other. It is the risk preference of the investor which determines the choice.

Stop-Loss Rule.   Whenever a position is entered, it should always be protected with a stop loss. A stop loss will change the performance profile, reducing both the size of the losses and the frequency of the

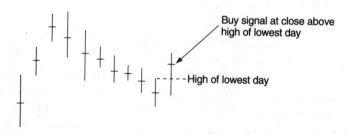

Figure 4–15   Entry rule for a buy signal based on the close that is higher than the high of the lowest day.

profitable trades. The primary difference between the swing break-out system and the 3-swing strategy is:

- In a 3-swing strategy we buy into a correction, while
- The swing breakout system uses a previous high as a buy entry point.

If both strategies work using the same stop-loss point, for example, a previous valley, then the 3-swing strategy has a much smaller risk because it is invested earlier. But, this may also result in more trades in the 3-swing strategy (Figure 4–16).

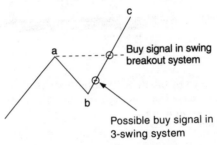

Figure 4–16 Example where we can have a buy signal in the 3-swing pattern compared to the swing breakout strategy.

Re-Entry Rule. Most often, trades are protected with a stop loss. If the stop loss is small, there are more situations where the position is stopped out. Once the trade has been stopped out it is necessary to decide whether or not to re-enter the market again or stand aside and wait for another new entry opportunity. A re-entry uses the original entry rule described above as long as the entry price is still above the swing low (for a long position).

Getting stopped out and re-entering the position can be painful and discouraging. But consistency is the most important part of trading. Elliott never discusses trading rules. It is the greatest weakness of the concept.

Profit Target Rule. Whenever a position is entered, a precalculated profit target should be entered simultaneously using the method described in Chapter 3.

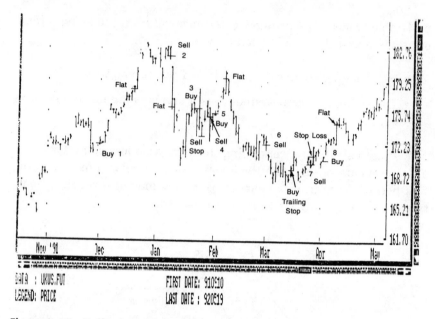

Figure 4–17 Daily chart of the British pound from 10-91 to 06-92. Buy/sell signals and profit targets based on the 3-swing pattern strategy. (*Source:* System Writer Plus, Omega Research, Inc.)

Trading Example. The following example uses the daily price chart for the British pound to show trading signals (Figure 4–17). The trading signals were generated using the following parameters:

- A swing size of 400 basis points,

- A minimum correction of 30%,

- An entry rule (buy) using the breakout of the previous high,

- A profit target of 0.618, and

- A stop loss of the 2-day previous low trailing stop.

With these parameters, the following trades would have been generated:

Trade #1	buy 171.90	sell 182.38	+10.48
Trade #2	sell 181.90	buy 176.10	+5.80
Trade #3	buy 176.20	sell 173.12	−3.08

Trade #4	sell 175.30	buy 175.70		−0.40
Trade #5	buy 175.70	sell 179.57	+3.87	
Trade #6	sell 172.36	buy 169.16	+3.20	
Trade #7	sell 170.16	buy 171.04		−0.88

For this limited example using the daily British pound chart, the comparison of the swing breakout system with the 3-swing system showed:

• Both systems had the same number of trades,

• The 3-swing system had smaller losses, and

• The breakout system had larger profits.

Although Elliott never mentioned an investment strategy such as this, it is based on his concept. It demonstrates that investing into retracements makes sense if the focus is on wave 3, and wave 5 is completely ignored. The combination of swing size, minimum correction, and entry rule seems to be a balanced strategy for daily and weekly data. The same strategy should work on intraday as well, but the parameters would have to be different.

A Very Short-Term Trading Approach

A short-term approach is meant to be an investment of not longer than one or two days. With a time span that short, very definitive rules are needed:

• When to enter,

• Where to place the stop loss, and

• Where to take profits.

There is no time to hesitate in this environment. The signals will come at those times when they are least expected. Entering the buy or sell order too late will result in big slippage and ultimately trading losses. This is especially true because products with a high volatility work well for fast systems, for the initial "thrust" is needed at the time of entry.

The secret is to enter the market at times when most of the speculators are still waiting, and to get out before the big volume "hits the trading floor." A strategy that can do this should give small but safe profits, resulting in a very stable equity curve.

Can such a strategy be developed from the Elliott/Fibonacci concept? We believe so. One way to approach such a strategy is to look at chart patterns that have a strong thrust in a given commodity. Conceptually, a short-term strategy can work with the following rules:

- Wait for a precalculated swing size and correction to be completed.

- Enter the market using an entry rule.

- Place a stop loss.

- Liquidate the position on the next day at a precalculated profit target.

- Liquidate on the close of next day.

When looking for fast moves, it is best to find commodities which are historically very trending and have high volatility. Over the past 17 years, these commodities include the British pound, Swiss franc, Deutsche mark, and Japanese yen. In this example, the British pound daily chart will be used, from October 10, 1991 through May 19, 1992, applying the following parameters.

Swing Size.   Looking for a 'thrust' requires a minimum swing size. To establish a new high swing for the daily British pound, the following conditions must be satisfied:

- A move of 400 basis points from the lowest low to the highest high.

- A low that is lower than the low of the highest day on either side of the highest high.

- A correction of at least 30% of the total move measured from the highest high (if the move is 500 points, a correction of at least 150 points is needed).

Once these criteria are fulfilled, a buy or sell entry occurs as shown in Figure 4–18.

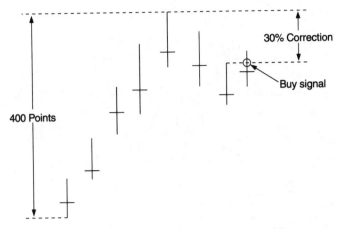

Figure 4–18   Three criteria for an entry rule.

Stop Loss.   If profit-taking is targeted for the day after the entry, the stop loss is placed at the previous day's low for a buy signal, and at the previous day's high for a sell signal. As an alternative, an intraday stop-loss strategy can be a good substitute for the daily stop. Again, remember that the most important factor is consistency. When taking quick profits, it is vital to be very rigid with the positioning and use of stops.

Profit Target.   To get the profit target, calculate:

- The average between the entry price and the highest high reached on the same day after the entry, or

- The average between the entry price and the lowest low reached on the days after entry.

The extreme highs and lows used to calculate the average exit prices are after the fact, and can never be reached. Based on the average figures it can be decided whether or not this strategy is worthwhile. If the average figure in a product is only 10 basis points, this strategy will not work. But with an average of 90 basis points as shown in the British pound, there is a very good chance of making profits. The individual trading signals generated by this short-term strategy are shown on the daily British pound chart in Figure 4–19.

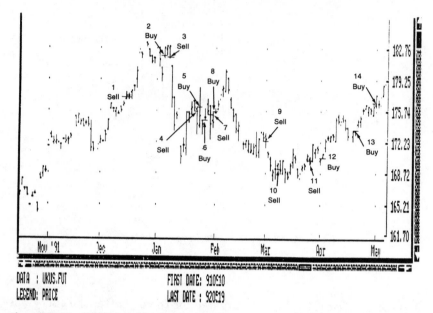

Figure 4–19 Daily British pound chart from 10-91 to 05-92. Buy/sell signals based on a very short-term trading approach. (*Source:* System Writer Plus, Omega Research, Inc.)

Computer Test Run. The test of the British pound covers the period from October, 1991 to June, 1992. The swings are marked in Figure 4–20 to make it easy to identify the individual trades. The test run shows:

- All swings,
- All entry signals,
- The maximum profit reached on the day of entry and three days later,
- The total number of trades, and
- The average number of basis points for all longs and shorts during the time period traded.

During this time period there were fifteen signals. On the day of entry, there are:

- An average profit of 92 basis points for the longs, and
- An average of 108 basis points for all shorts.

```
CommNum      26 Calc dates from  911121 to  920519
Swing size  from   4.00  to   5.00
Retracement from   30.00% to 100.00%
```

```
=========================== Swing Size Report ==========================

911202 172.80 : SwingLow  from   175.40 to   170.80  43.48%   4.60 pts
920103 178.90 : SwingHigh from   170.80 to   183.46  36.02%  12.66 pts
920106 182.84 : SwingLow  from   183.46 to   178.90  86.40%   4.56 pts
920108 181.60 : SwingHigh from   178.90 to   182.90  32.50%   4.00 pts
920117 175.70 : SwingLow  from   182.96 to   169.70  45.25%  13.26 pts
920123 173.12 : SwingHigh from   169.70 to   176.80  51.83%   7.10 pts
920127 173.10 : SwingHigh from   173.12 to   178.40 100.38%   5.28 pts
920128 176.00 : SwingLow  from   178.40 to   173.10  54.72%   5.30 pts
920130 172.50 : SwingHigh from   173.10 to   177.10 115.00%   4.00 pts
920131 175.70 : SwingLow  from   177.10 to   172.50  69.57%   4.60 pts
920210 177.77 : SwingHigh from   172.50 to   180.40  33.29%   7.90 pts
920227 173.58 : SwingLow  from   180.40 to   170.40  31.80%  10.00 pts
920306 170.28 : SwingLow  from   173.58 to   167.96  41.28%   5.62 pts
920323 169.70 : SwingLow  from   171.50 to   167.32  56.94%   4.18 pts
920401 169.78 : SwingHigh from   167.32 to   172.06  48.10%   4.74 pts
920415 173.60 : SwingHigh from   169.78 to   175.54  33.68%   5.76 pts
920430 175.22 : SwingHigh from   172.30 to   176.58  31.78%   4.28 pts
920508 177.24 : SwingHigh from   175.22 to   179.30  50.49%   4.08 pts
```

```
==================== Profitability Report ====================

      Date   Pos   Entry      0      1
      911209 SE   175.80   0.30,   0.80   175.74,
      920106 LE   181.70   1.14,   1.20   182.80,
      920108 SE   181.88   0.28,   5.88   177.06,
      920123 SE   175.68   2.56,   1.88   175.16,
      920124 LE   176.22   2.18,  -1.42   174.14,
      920128 LE   174.84   1.16,   2.26   175.62,
      920130 SE   175.28   7.78,   1.48   174.44,
      920203 LE   175.72   0.26,   1.18   176.30,
      920302 SE   172.34   0.72,   1.94   170.80,
      920310 SE   169.20   0.50,   0.64   170.12,
      920326 SE   170.12   0.42,  -0.02   172.02,
      920402 LE   170.50   0.50,   2.10   172.38,
      920421 LE   173.52   0.12,   1.48   174.56,
      920501 LE   176.72   0.78,   0.48   176.58,
      920512 LE   179.22   1.18,   2.50   181.50,

      Trades        bar 0              bar 1
                cnt Total  per     cnt Total  per
      Long :     8  7.32 0.915,     8  9.78 1.223,
      Short:     7  7.56 1.080,     7 12.60 1.800,

CommNum      26 Calc dates from  911121 to  920519 for      124 bars.
Swing size  from   4.00  to   5.00
Retracement from   30.00% to 100.00%
```

Figure 4-20   Computer test-run explaining the buy and sell signals as shown in Figure 4-19. (*Source:* System Writer Plus, Omega Research, Inc.)

Slippage and commissions were not included. This example demonstrates that working with retracements can make a lot of sense for the very short-term oriented investor. Conceptually this strategy can be used with intraday data as well. It is very demanding on the investor, for it requires high accuracy. This analysis works because of the "thrust" that occurs at special entry points. Every commodity is different. Experience shows that the best results are achieved in products with high liquidity. The major currencies or bonds are excellent candidates.

BIG CORRECTIONS AND TREND CHANGES

"Big trend changes" are meant to be corrections of 50% to 62%. This is based on a swing size of at least 10 full points (e.g., 60.00–70.00) for the Deutsche mark, Swiss franc, and Japanese yen. The problem with corrections is that we can never know exactly how far they might go. Even though they may often stop in the range 50% to 62%, they may retrace as far as the beginning of the previous peak or valley.

To get more control over the corrections, the following rules can be used.

Entry Rule

The entry rule follows the same logic described earlier. A buy signal occurs when the close is higher than the high of the lowest day, or a previous peak is broken, whichever comes first (the opposite for a sell signal).

Stop-Loss Rule

As with any other strategy, a position is never entered without placing a stop loss. The stop-loss rule is the same as that described earlier.

Re-Entry Rule

Whenever a trade is stopped out, it should be re-entered when the criteria for the entry rule has been fulfilled again.

Profit Target Rule

Because corrections of 50% or more on weekly charts are far away from previous peaks or valleys, it is not necessary to wait for a 3-swing move as described in the section on "short-term investments." The profit target is expected to be a retracement of at least 50% of the total correction move. Figure 4–21 shows the expected retracement. The profit target is calculated as 50% of the total amplitude between A and B (the vertical distance or price difference).

Trailing Stop

Trailing stops have already been described as a good strategy for participating in the expected price moves. They are an alternative to the

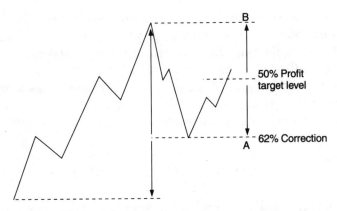

Figure 4–21   50% Profit target after a 62% correction.

profit targets. The choice of strategy depends on the risk preference of the investor and the market conditions.

Chart Examples

In the weekly chart of the Deutsche mark, shown in Figure 4–22, a 62% retracement was reached three times. They occurred at points *A*, *B*, and *C*. At points *A* and *B*, the market price went slightly over the price targets. The market trend changed precisely at point *C*.

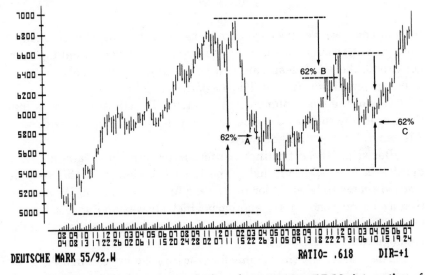

DEUTSCHE MARK 55/92.W   RATIO= .618   DIR=+1

Figure 4–22   Weekly Deutsche mark chart from 08-89 to 07-92. Integration of 62% corrections.

Using the rules given for a big correction, a trade could have been entered when a new swing high and low occurred. The trader had the choice of liquidating the positions at the profit targets, or could have used trailing stops as an alternative.

The signals in Figure 4–22 show the profit potential and the risk exposure of this strategy. It also shows how the entry rule prevented the position from being set too early.

USE OF THE OPTIONS MARKET

When long-term goals are reached in weekly or daily charts, options on futures become a good investment tool. By using options the trading risk can be limited, and yet we can still participate in the expected move. If an option is bought with a strike price *at* the money or *in* the money and an expiration date at least a full three months away, an option will work as a low-risk substitute.

When working with corrections, options strategies should only be used after big price swings, and then for corrections of at least 50%. A big correction can only be expected in conjunction with a large or highly volatile swing. This situation makes the use of options practical.

SUMMARY

In this chapter, we discussed corrections in detail. The problem of working with corrections is one of patience. Whenever a trending market exists, there is a desperate fear of missing the trend, and a desire to participate immediately. The opposite should be true.

One of the most interesting aspects of the Elliott concept is that there are numerous 3-waves moves in any market situation. And, wave 3 is generally the strongest wave.

Based on these findings, different investment strategies were discussed. It was shown, using the British pound, that the 3-swing method seems to be superior to a swing breakout system. We also introduced a very short-term approach which showed an interesting performance profile of very small losses. Such a strategy only works if the slippage can be controlled.

The shorter the time frame for trading, the more demanding the strategy, and the more discipline is needed.

There are two different techniques when working with corrections. We can focus on being invested as much as possible, trying to never miss a trend. For this approach we described a balance between swing size, correction, and entry rule. The other choice is to wait for safer entry points, offered by corrections of 50% to 62% "big" swings. For this choice we gave rules to use when major price targets are reached.

Options on futures were mentioned again as a reasonable alternative strategy when a 62% correction of a big swing size is reached.

The wave count was ignored in this chapter. The complexity of corrections is so great that there does not seem to be any value in attempting to forecast whether a 5-wave price move will occur.

5

WORKING WITH EXTENSIONS

Extensions are exuberant price movements. They express themselves in run-away markets, opening gaps, limit up and limit down moves, and high volatility. These situations can offer good trading potential if the analysis is carried out in accordance with sensible and definitive rules.

Elliott noted, "Extensions may appear in any one of the 3 impulse waves, but in never more than one" (p. 55). This is shown in Figures 5–1 and 5–2.

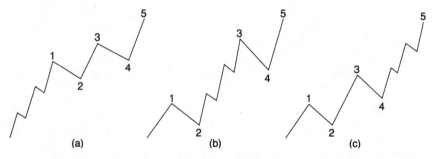

Figure 5–1   (a) Extension in wave in uptrend; (b) extension in wave 3 in uptrend; (c) extension in wave 5 in uptrend.

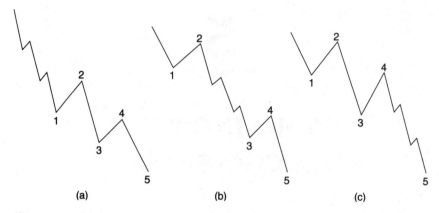

Figure 5-2 (a) Extension in wave 1 in downtrend; (b) extension in wave 3 in downtrend; (c) extension in wave 5 in downtrend.

"On rare occasions there are a total of 9 waves, all of almost equal size" (Elliott, p. 55). This is shown in Figure 5-3.

To fine-tune his strategy Elliott added, "Extensions are double retraced, that is, a correction will pass over the same ground twice. If the extension occurs in wave 3, double correction will take care of wave 4 and wave 5" (p. 55) (see Figure 5-4).

The correction after a fifth wave extension has already been discussed in Chapter 4. Figure 5-5 shows the fifth wave correction.

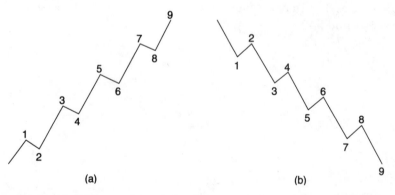

Figure 5-3 (a) 9 Waves of equal size in uptrend; (b) 9 waves of equal size in downtrend.

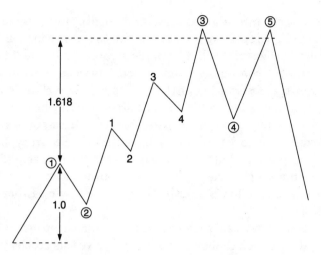

Figure 5-4   Ratio 1.618 used with the amplitude of wave 1 to calculate the price band for the end of wave 5.

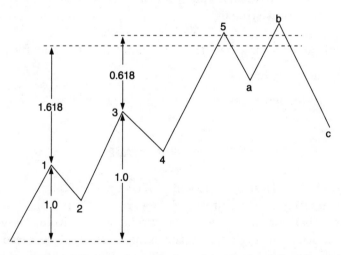

Figure 5-5   Ratio 1.618 is used to calculate the price band for wave 5 with the amplitude of wave 1. Ratio 0.618 is used to calculate the price band for wave 5 with the amplitude of wave 3.

Elliott performed a great service by identifying extensions and putting them in perspective with respect to the wave count. But in doing so, there is a complete change in his strategy. Elliott claims that, by mastering his concept, we can forecast price moves in advance. Even though the observation of the extensions as a chart pattern is brilliant, it is not a forecasting tool. Forecasting means that, if the current price is 60.00, we anticipate that it will go for example, to 70.00. We do not believe this is possible with high accuracy, but what we will try to prove is that, if the price reaches the precalculated level of 70.00, then a short trade can be entered anticipating a price reversal to the downside. This is exactly the opposite of what Elliott followers try to do.

Elliott never worked with extensions as an independent trading tool. It could have been that he was unable to solve this problem because his focus was fixed on the wave count. Again, it is not the wave count that makes the Elliott concept work, but the Fibonacci sequence with its ratio 1.618. But, the results are better when both are used together. Extensions can be seen in intraday, daily, weekly, or monthly charts; the longer the extension, the bigger the profit potential. On the other hand, it might take weeks or months to get a signal. Extensions can occur in an uptrend, downtrend, or in any kind of market condition. In order to work with extensions successfully it is necessary to have a balanced strategy consisting of:

- A minimum swing size (the wave count is not important),

- The ratio 1.618, and

- Entry and exit rules.

EXTENSIONS IN WAVE 3

Elliott said, "The first retracement will occur immediately in 3 waves to approximately the beginning of the extension" (p. 18). Elliott observed another characteristic of the extension in wave 3, "When the movement occurs at high speed, the same territory is retraced at almost the same speed in reverse" (p. 57).

The extensions in wave 3 can be seen on the daily soybean chart in Figure 5–6. Once the precalculated price goal is reached (wave 1 times 1.618), a strong correction follows.

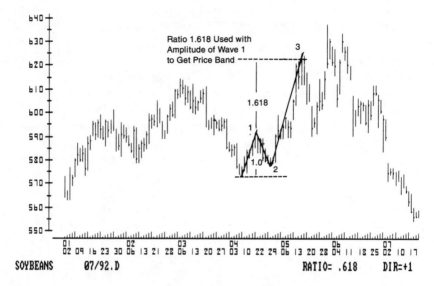

Figure 5–6   Daily soybean chart from 01-02 to 07-92. The ratio 1.618 is used to calculate the end of the extension of wave 3 with the amplitude of wave 1.

To calculate price targets in the extension of wave 3, the following steps are needed:

1. Measure the total amplitude of wave 1: $5.93 − 5.74 + $0.19

2. Multiply the swing size of wave 1 times 1.618: $0.19 × 1.618 = $ .31

3. Add: $5.93 + .31 = $6.24

Then the precalculated price target for the third wave extension was $6.39 per bushel. Figure 5–6 shows that the market price went to $6.41 and then dropped in a free fall to $6.05.

When analyzing extensions, the same problems occur that were seen in the retracement analysis. These are that the market price:

• Comes close to the precalculated price, but misses by a small margin.

• Reaches the precalculated price exactly.

• Overshoots the precalculated price by a small margin.

Figure 5–7 shows the three possibilities.

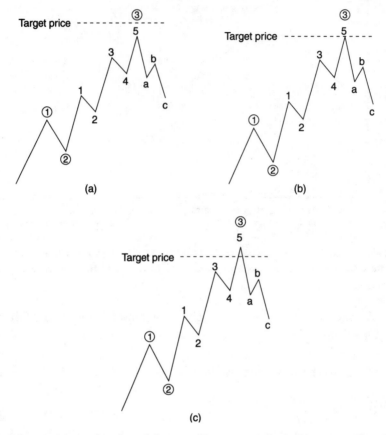

Figure 5–7 (a) Target price of the extension not reached; (b) target price of the extension reached; (c) market price higher than the precalculated target price.

A trader must accept the premise that there is no perfect entry point. To work with this assumption, the following sections define the necessary rules.

Swing Size

A minimum swing size is needed to make this strategy work. If the swing size is *too small* then:

- There is too much noise, causing the swings to be unpredictable.

- The corrections do not offer enough profit potential.

Figure 5–8   Four examples for a successful minimum swing.

- There is a greater chance that the price goals precalculated from the ratio 1.618 will be unreliable.

- The minimum swing size recommended for the Deutsche mark, Japanese yen, and Swiss franc is 200 basis points, and 400 points for the British pound.

If the swing size is too big, then there are very few occurrences of the extension formation on weekly or monthly charts. However, when they do appear they offer good profit potential.

To confirm a swing high it is necessary to have:

- An upswing of at least the minimum swing size (e.g., 200 basis points for the Swiss franc). The wave count is not used.

- A confirmation of the high, given as a close that is lower than the low of the highest day.

Figure 5–8 shows four examples of a successful minimum swing.

In addition, there must be a 38% minimum correction following the highest day (as in Figure 5–9), and a low that is lower than the low of the highest day (Figure 5–10).

Figure 5–9   Minimum swing size with 38% correction.

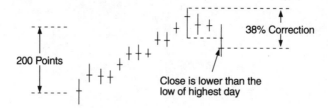

Figure 5–10 Minimum swing size with 38% correction and the close that is lower than the low of the highest day.

Fibonacci Ratio

From the Fibonacci Summation Series, the ratios 0.618, 1.0, and 1.618 were introduced. These were applied to the length of the previous swing (see Figure 5–11). Of these three ratios, we will only work with the ratio 1.618. This is the ratio that represents "Nature's Law" and best expresses human behavior, as discussed in Chapter 1.

There is no rationale behind this ratio. Moves are triggered by news, crop or storage reports, political or economic events, but emotions take over. Greed, fear, fast markets, and stop-loss orders cause the extreme price swings.

Entry Rule

By integrating the entry rule, the investment strategy can be fine-tuned. When the trade is to sell or buy into an extension, protection is needed in the event the trend reverses. Although the entry rule takes away part of the profit potential, the trade becomes much safer.

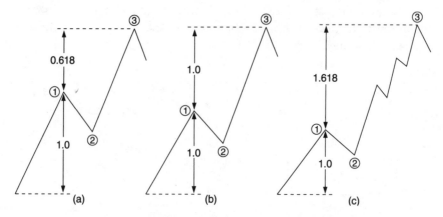

Figure 5–11 (a) Ratio 0.618; (b) ratio 1.0; (c) ratio 1.618.

Whenever the price target is reached on a daily chart, a short position is entered if the previous two lows are broken (which must also include the low of the highest day), or if the close is lower than the low of the highest day, whichever comes first (the opposite for a buy signal). These two cases are shown in Figure 5–12.

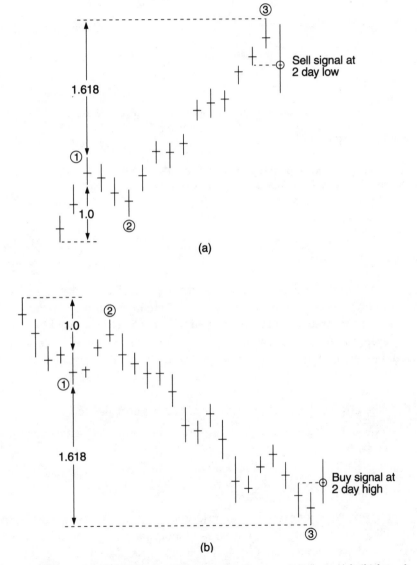

Figure 5–12 (a) Sell signal after the extension in wave 3 in uptrend; (b) buy signal after the extension in wave 3 in downtrend.

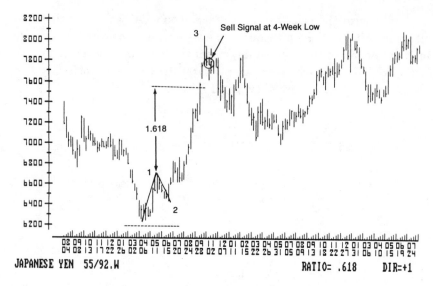

Figure 5–13 Weekly Japanese yen chart from 07-89 to 06-92. Sell signal after an extension in the wave 3 after a 4-week low is broken.

The entry rule is a very important part of the strategy when working with extensions. There is always a chance that the price will overshoot the precalculated price goal. Figure 5–13, the weekly chart of the Japanese yen, shows the case where the entry rule served as valuable protection against entering the market too early. A short position would be entered after the price target is reached if:

- The close is lower than the low of the highest day, or
- The price breaks the last four previous lows, whichever comes first.

Stop-Loss Rule

When a position is entered, it should always be protected with a stop loss. The rule is that, after entering a short position, a stop is placed one tick above the previous high. For longs, it is placed one tick below the previous low. Figure 5–14 shows the location of the stops.

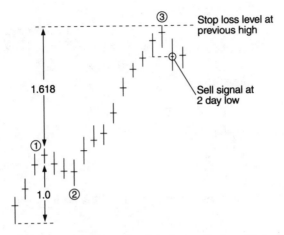

Figure 5–14   Stop loss level is placed 1 tick above previous high after sell signal.

Re-Entry Rule

Whether the trade is to be re-entered after being stopped out depends on the swing size of wave 1. There is no re-entry if the amplitude of wave 1 is about 200 points or less, for the daily Deutsche mark, Swiss franc, or Japanese yen. The rationale is that a small swing increases the chances of the trend continuing in wave 5.

A re-entry is favored if the amplitude of wave 1 is greater than 400 points (twice the minimum swing move) for those same currencies. By analyzing extensions, it turns out that price targets based on a large first wave seem to be safer than price targets from a smaller first wave. Following Elliott, every extension will be double retraced. If the trade is stopped out, the cause may very well be the irregular top or bottom of corrective wave *b*. Most of the time the stronger wave *c* will follow in the original trend direction. This move can only be caught by re-entering the position. Re-entering seems to be safer when the price move in the extension is large. The re-entry rule is the same as the entry rule (Figure 5–15).

The re-entry signal is based on the amplitude of wave 1 because the magnitude of wave 3 must be big enough to expect a correspondingly big correction. Normally, these large swings in wave 1 can only be seen on weekly charts. They do not occur often, but if they can be identified in a timely manner, they offer very good profit potential.

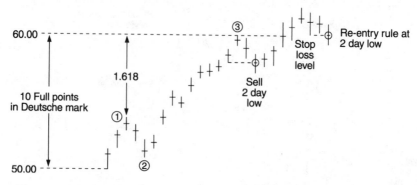

Figure 5–15   Re-entry rule after a sell signal the position got stopped out.

The bigger swing size also works in favor of the re-entry signal. The chances that the market has exhausted itself after a very strong, straight move is much greater than after a smaller move. The swing size is also important for the profit target.

Profit Targets

Whenever a position is entered, the precalculated profit target should also be entered. The profit target is 50% of the total distance from the start of wave 1 to the end of wave 3. Once this target is reached, the position is closed out and the trader must wait for another opportunity. The 50% rule is not computer-tested, but a value commonly used in chart analysis. This is shown in Figure 5–16.

How is the profit target calculated? Using the 3-swing pattern in Figure 5–16, note the start of wave 1 at point $A = 70.00,$ and the end of wave 3 at point $B = 54.00$. To calculate the profit target, take 50% of the distance from A to B and add it to the low at point B.

Start of wave 1 minus end of wave 3	$70.00 - 54.00 = 16.00$
Take 50% of the distance	$A - B = 8.00$
Then the profit target is	62.00

The long position is closed out when it reaches 62.00. No position is entered until the rules offer a new opportunity. Figure 5–17 demonstrates the sequence of events in this strategy.

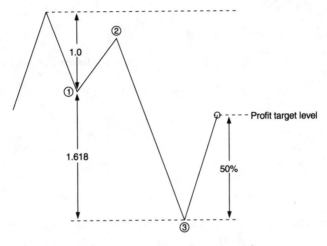

Figure 5–16   50% Profit target rule.

Trailing Stops

Whenever a position is entered, a trailing stop may be used as an alternative to the profit target. When the price goals are reached in a third-wave extension, a fast correction is normally expected. When working with daily data, this means that the trade should be profitable shortly after it is initiated.

By placing the trailing stop (for a short position) at the high of the previous two days, profits are protected without eliminating all of the opportunity of participating in a trending market. The negative of this strategy is that it increases the chances of getting stopped out

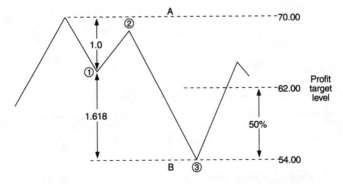

Figure 5–17   Calculation of profit target level.

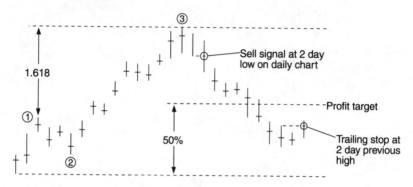

Figure 5–18   Integration of trailing stops.

before the profit target is reached. The strategies can be combined by using the profit target, then switching over to the trailing stop once the profit target is reached (Figure 5–18).

The daily chart of the British pound (Figure 5–19) offers a good example of how to work with extensions. The entry signal occurs at point *A,* and the trailing stop is at point *B.*

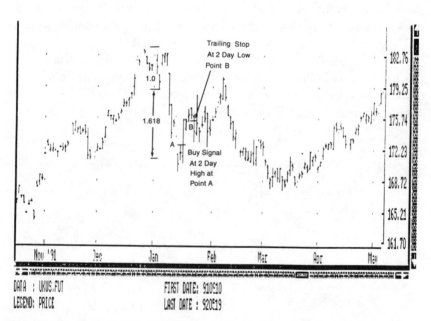

Figure 5–19   Daily British pound chart from 08-91 to 03-92. Example for the extension in wave 3. Entry rule at point A trailing stop at point B.

EXTENSIONS IN WAVE 5

In searching for safe entry points, the end of the extension in wave 5, in combination with the double retracement, offers a good possibility. The only disadvantage is that is happens very seldom. Elliott wrote, "It will be noted that in each instance there is a total of 9 waves, counting the extended wave 5 instead of 1" (p. 55). In this special case we are only interested in the extension of wave 5, as shown in Figure 5–20.

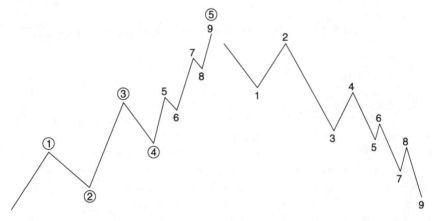

Figure 5–20   Extension in wave 5.

Elliott also observed a very special case when he said, "On rare occasions an extended movement will be composed of 9 waves, all of equal size" (p. 55). This is shown in Figure 5–21.

Elliott made a very important observation when he noticed, "Extensions in wave 5 have a double retracement" (p. 56). This is shown in Figure 5–22.

If there is one point considered the safe opportunity, this is the one. If only we have the patience to wait for it. This case requires waiting for two separate events:

1. We must first be very lucky to identify an extension in wave 5.

2. After it has been identified, we must wait for the double retracement.

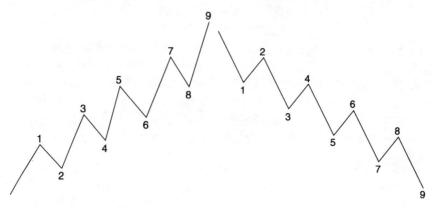

Figure 5–21   Extended movement of 9 waves of equal size.

A picture book case for such a pattern is the daily chart of the Japanese yen, shown in Figure 5–23.

In this figure there is a perfect 9-wave count and the double retracement, as forecasted by Elliott. If any of Elliott's patterns have forecasting value, this is it. Elliott never mentioned anything about swing size, ratio, or entry/exit rules. After explaining Elliott's use of the trend channel, we have added these missing rules to give definitive entry and exit points.

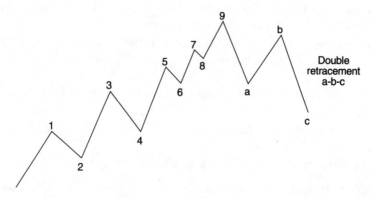

Figure 5–22   Double retracement after a 5-swing move.

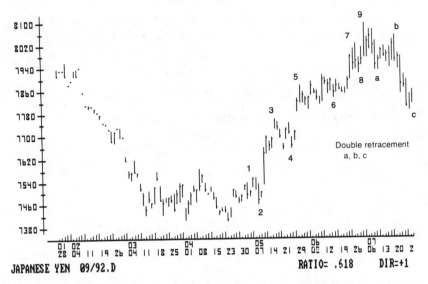

Figure 5–23   Daily Japanese yen chart from 02-92 to 07-92. After a move of almost 9 equal swings followed a double retracement of an a-b-c correction.

Trend Channel

Elliott solved the problem of identifying the end of the extension in wave 5 by using the semi-logarithmic chart. Once the upper trendline is touched, the trend should reverse.

One of Elliott's most important discoveries is reflected in the statement, "When 5 waves upward have been completed, 3 waves down will follow" (p. 112). He also said, "Extensions may appear in any one of the 3 impulses, i.e., waves 1, 3, or 5, but never more than in one" (p. 55). This means that once an extension in wave 5 is identified, there is a strong indication that a trend change is due. This is shown in Figure 5–24.

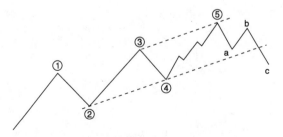

Figure 5–24   Trend change after a 5-wave cycle.

In summary, there are three criteria which can be found in the Elliott concept, that should identify where the trend will change:

1. The extension in wave 5.

2. A penetration of the semi-log trendline.

3. An *a-b-c* correction indicating the trend change.

But even with these points Elliott still did not say:

- At what point to enter the market.

- Where to place a stop loss.

- Where to re-enter when the trade is stopped out.

- When to take profits.

An investment strategy exists only when all these parts work together. Elliott did, for example, identify the appearance of the *a-b-c* correction at the end of wave 5. But, is it a simple, double, or triple complex correction? The following rules are introduced to turn Elliott's concept into a useful trading strategy.

Fibonacci Ratio

When working with the extension in wave 3, multiply the amplitude of wave 1 by the Fibonacci ratio 1.618 to get the price goal for the end of wave 3. This is shown in Figure 5–25.

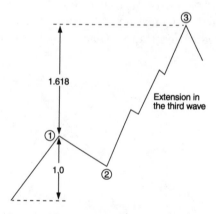

Figure 5–25   The ratio 1.618 is used to calculate the end of wave 3 with the amplitude of wave 1.

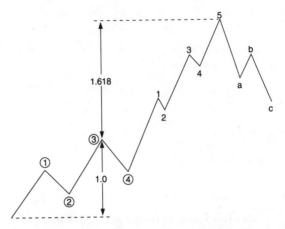

Figure 5–26   The ratio 1.618 is used to calculate the end of wave 5 with the amplitude from the beginning of wave 1 to the top of wave 3.

When working with the extension in wave 5, multiply the total amplitude from the beginning of wave 1 to the top of wave 3 by the Fibonacci ration 1.618 to get the price goal for the end of wave 5. This can be seen in Figure 5–26.

Entry Rule

In order to work with the extension in wave 5, it is necessary to identify that extension as well as the *a-b* correction. A short position is entered by selling one tick below the valley formed by wave *a* and *b*, (the opposite of a buy signal). This is illustrated in Figure 5–27.

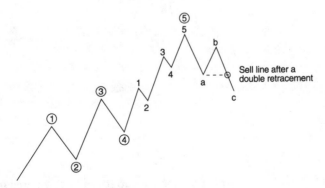

Figure 5–27   Sell signal after the end of a 5-wave cycle and the double retracement.

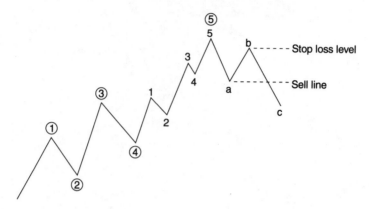

Figure 5–28   The stop loss is placed for a short signal above the previous peak.

Stop-Loss Rule

Following the very conservative approach provided by the entry rule, there is only a small chance that the position will be stopped out. But we cannot know whether the *a-b-c* correction that has been entered is going to be a normal, double, or triple correction. To protect the position, a stop loss is placed (for a short) above the previous peak, formed between wave *b* and wave *c*. This is shown in Figure 5–28.

Re-Entry Signal

Should the position be stopped out, it can be re-entered by following the regular entry rule, as shown in Figure 5–29.

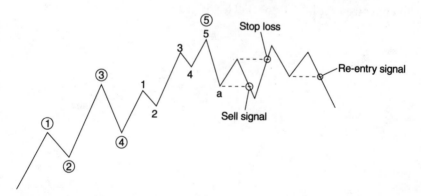

Figure 5–29   Should the position be stopped out, it can be re-entered following the regular entry rule.

USING THE OPTIONS MARKET

Options on futures can be used as a valid strategy in the extension of wave 3 and wave 5 if the total amplitude of the price swing in the underlying futures contract is big enough. For example, in the Deutsche mark, Swiss franc, and Japanese yen the end of wave 3 or wave 5 should be at least 10 full points (70.00 to 80.00). When buying puts or calls, the following must be applied:

- Puts or calls can be bought as an alternative to an outright short or long futures position.

- The strike price should be either "at the money" or "in the money." This keeps the premium to a reasonable level.

- The expiration date should be at least three trading months away.

- The option is liquidated when the profit targets are reached.

SUMMARY

In this chapter, we discussed extensions in detail. The greatest problem is waiting for the end of the extension before entering a position.

We discussed the difference between an extension in wave 3 and wave 5. An investment at the end of the extension of wave 5 can be considered the safest entry point of all. An investment at the end of the extension of wave 5 can be considered the safest point in the Elliott concept, if the strategies are combined with entry and exit rules.

Identifying extensions was discussed in detail. Even though rules were defined that filtered out many of the situations within the Elliott concept, there is still room for caution.

Elliott mentioned that there is only one extension possible in a 5-wave pattern, while he also wrote, "This is the first time in my observation that two extensions ever registered in one cycle" (Elliott p. 171).

The statement that extensions only occur in the direction of the main trend becomes relative when Elliott writes, "Insofar as records are available, an extension has never occurred in the direction opposite to the current main trend, therefore further developments will have to define what the implication may be" (p. 165).

Extensions happen in run-away markets. It is not possible to know in advance when they will occur. They are exuberant price moves which happen when investors or speculators get caught by surprise. Unexpected economic data, crop reports, storage figures or extreme weather forecasts can cause "fast" markets with gap openings and limit moves. Fear and greed, combined with stop orders, might increase the volatility of a market.

The price goals can be calculated with the Fibonacci ratio 1.618.

Investing into extensions is difficult, because positions are contrary to the market trend. Extensions and retracements are part of the overall Elliott/Fibonacci concept. If both turn at the same point, it can be considered a safer investment.

6

MULTIPLE FIBONACCI PRICE TARGETS

The previous chapters have tried to show that the precalculated price targets based on the 5-wave pattern are a good indication of where the trend will change. But there are also times when prices overshoot or do not reach the price goals.

COMBINING DAILY 5-WAVE PATTERNS AND WEEKLY CORRECTIONS

By combining parts of the Elliott concept with Fibonacci ratios, we tried to improve the overall investment approach. Historical intraday, daily, weekly, and/or monthly charts were used to identify different elements of the wave patterns and the Fibonacci ratios.

Using daily and weekly charts, this chapter will analyze the combination of Elliott and Fibonacci applied to:

- The 5-wave pattern,

- Extensions, and

- Corrections.

Integrating Time Spans

Elliott recognized the importance of integrating different time spans when he wrote, "In fast markets the daily range is essential and the hourly useful, if not always essential. On the contrary, when the daily range becomes obscure, due to slow speed and long duration of the waves, condensation into weekly range clarifies" (p. 139). Figure 6–1 shows the integration of hourly, daily, and weekly data (Elliott, p. 147).

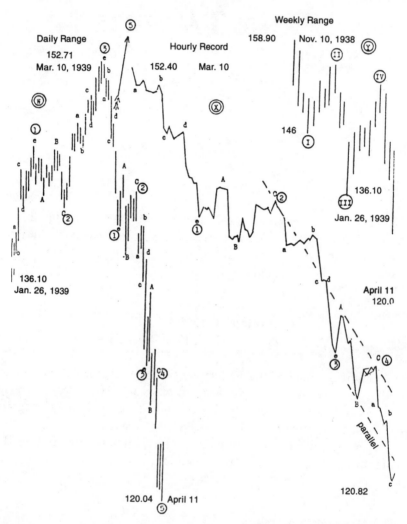

Figure 6–1 Dow Jones Industrial average original Elliott daily chart from 01-1939 to 04-1939.

Inclusion of Fibonacci

While it seems that Elliott concentrated most of his energy on the wave count, Fibonacci ratios now appear to be more important. Elliott tried to integrate Fibonacci into his wave count when he wrote, "Later I found that the basis of my discoveries was a Law of Nature known to the designers of the Great Pyramid of Gizeh which may have been constructed 5,000 years ago" (p. 42).

The Law of Nature to which Elliott is referring must be the Fibonacci summation series with its ratio 1.618. This is the figure that can be found throughout the pyramid of Gizeh, not the complex wave patterns in the Elliott concept. The way we read Elliott's work is that he used the appeal of the Fibonacci summation series as a marketing tool. But in all his analyses, he barely used the Fibonacci ratios. In all of Elliott's original letters that were made available to us, there was not one buy or sell signal strictly generated from the Fibonacci ratio.

The better approach is to use the Fibonacci ratios with the Elliott concept to precalculate price targets. When the ratio 1.618 (62%) has priority over the wave count, definitive trading rules can be developed. There should also be a priority in the importance of the price goals:

1. A 62% weekly correction is more important than the 5-wave daily pattern.

2. A 62% daily correction is more important than the 5-wave intra-day pattern.

Large, longer term corrections have preference over shorter-term patterns. This is shown in Figure 6–2.

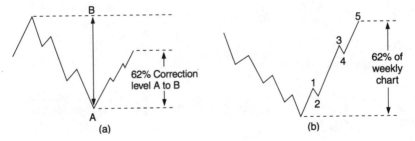

Figure 6–2 (a) 62% correction level on a weekly chart; (b) 5-wave cycle on a daily chart.

Whenever there is a 62 % correction on the weekly chart, follow the rules established in Chapter 4. Big weekly corrections, for example, 10 full points in the Swiss franc (60.00–70.00), will automatically have a multiple wave count on the daily chart. The combination of the weekly and daily chart has the following advantages: A 62% correction on the weekly chart warns of a trend change, and the integration of the daily chart helps to fine-tune the entry signals.

Swiss Franc Example

Weekly Chart.   In the weekly chart of the Swiss franc (Figure 6–3), the price move from points A to B was followed by a correction of a little more than 62%. All the rules described in Chapter 4 concerning corrections would have worked. A short position would have been entered at 73.65 by adhering to the entry rule.

For the purposes of review, the entry rule applied to "corrections and big trend changes" is: *Once the price targets are reached, buy if the close is higher than the high of the lowest day.*

The price move from B to C was corrected by more than 62%. All the rules given for corrections would have worked here as well. A long position would have been entered at 66.20, according to the rules.

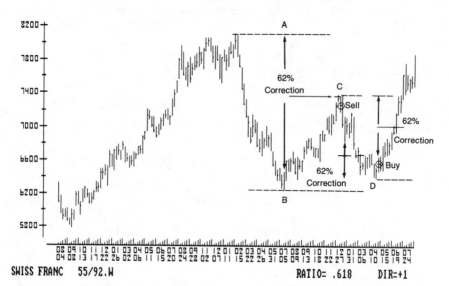

Figure 6–3   Weekly Swiss franc chart from 08-89 to 08-92. Sell signal after a 62% correction. Buy signal after a 62% correction.

Daily Chart.   Figure 6–4 shows the daily chart of the Swiss franc. At the time when the 62% correction between point C and D was reached in the weekly chart, the daily chart had a near-perfect 5-wave pattern. Returning to the entry rule for the 5-wave pattern, in Chapter 4, we have to wait for wave *a* and wave *b* to be completed, then we sell into wave *c*. Additional requirements for a sell signal are:

1. A minimum swing size of 100 points for the daily Swiss franc,

2. A close that is lower than the low of the lowest day to confirm the swing size, and

3. A correction of at least the minimum swing size (100 points) to confirm the high.

On the daily chart (Figure 6–4) there is no confirmation for the sell signal at the weekly 62% correction level.

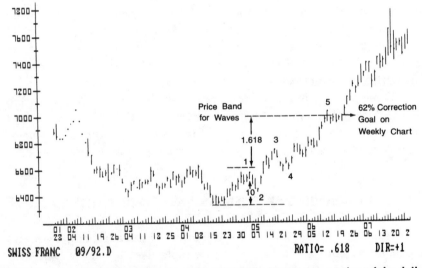

SWISS FRANC   09/92.D   RATIO= .618   DIR=+1

Figure 6–4   Daily Swiss franc chart from 01-92 to 08-92. Integration of the daily chart into the weekly Swiss franc chart.

Summary Analysis

This example shows the integration of daily and weekly data with the entry and exit rules described in Chapter 4. It shows the weakness of the Elliott concept and the improvement that can be made by integrating simple but necessary trading rules.

If the decision had been based only on the 5-wave pattern of the daily chart, without an entry rule, we could have sold at 140.50. Under normal circumstances a correction could have been expected on the downside. But exactly the opposite happened.

After the fact, it was clear that a very rare 9-wave pattern occurred, with nine almost identical waves. Once these nine waves were completed, the anticipated strong correction finally followed. Were the investors still waiting when it came?

"On rare occasions an extended movement will be composed of 9 waves, all of equal size" (Elliott, p. 55). But in order to base the entry decision on the wave count alone, we must know the count in advance or forecast the move based on the Elliott wave patterns. How can this be done? We never know in advance what pattern will develop and will therefore not know our market position in advance, either in an uptrend or downtrend.

This example questions another statement of Elliott, "Extensions occur only in new territory of the current cycle. That is they do not occur in corrections" (p. 55). The weekly Swiss franc chart calls for the following interpretation: The market is in the correction of the move from A to B, and the extension occurred, not in new territory, but within a correction.

Some Elliott followers might totally disagree with our wave count. Time will show what happens. Because Elliott did not offer any mechanical rules that can be applied to his concept, the door is open for independent analysis.

COMBINING EXTENSIONS AND CORRECTIONS

Extensions and corrections can be combined on intraday, daily, weekly, and monthly charts. The following example uses a weekly Deutsche mark chart.

The safest entry points are where the Fibonacci price goals are close together. If there is a price band (the range formed by price goals), the entry rule is applied when the first line of the price band is penetrated.

In the analysis of the weekly Deutsche mark chart, the price goals for the corrections are used first, followed by the price goals for the extensions. This is shown in Figure 6–5.

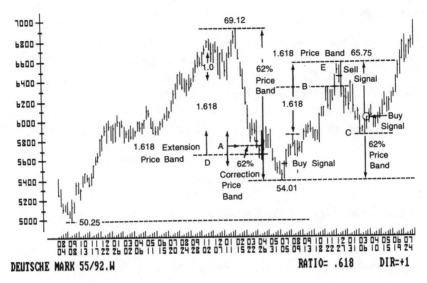

Figure 6-5 Weekly Deutsche mark chart from 08–89 to 08–92. Integration of price targets of extensions and corrections.

There are three major swings on the chart:

1. From 50.25 to 69.12,

2. From 69.12 to 54.01, and

3. From 54.01 to 65.75.

Corrections

In Chapter 4, corrections were described in detail—when they happen and what to look for. In the weekly Deutsche mark chart, a 62 % correction was reached three times, at points A, B, and C. At points A and B the market price went slightly over the price targets, while the trend changed precisely at point C. Using the rules developed for corrections, the following sequence of events would have occurred:

- A market entry following the entry rules (close above the high of the low day for a buy signal, vice versa for a sell signal).

- Either profits could have been taken at the profit targets, or, profits would have been taken using a trailing stop.

Extensions

Continuing with the rules previously defined in Chapter 4, extensions can be found to have occurred at points D and E.

At point D the market went lower than the extension goal, but the entry rule prevented us from entering too early.

At point E the market precisely reached the price targeting the end of the extension and then turned around.

SUMMARY

In the weekly chart of the Deutsche mark, the analysis shows:

- Every time the precalculated price targets are reached, a major trend change followed, either immediately or shortly afterward.

- It is not clear whether the price target for extensions or corrections are more important; therefore, both should be weighted equally.

- Whenever a price target for a long-term extension or correction is reached, we continue to wait for the entry rule. In most cases, this is the confirmation of the trend change.

- Other trading rules were re-enforced:

  —Always work with a stop loss.

  —Re-enter if stopped out.

  —Use profit targets or trailing stops, whichever is preferred by the investor.

As an additional strategy, the entry rule can be changed to wait for the double retracement described in Chapter 3.

Price goals based on the combination of extensions and corrections do not require a wave count or wave pattern to be recognized.

7

TIME ANALYSIS

During the Elliott/Fibonacci seminars, held by the author in 1983 in the United States, we introduced a trading concept strictly based on *Fibonacci time analysis.* Today this concept is as sound as it was then. Only now it's computerized. The performance profile has not changed. It can be shown that Fibonacci ratios are a reliable and consistent tool for time analysis and should be integrated into an investment strategy.

Fibonacci ratios can be applied to any commodity or time span. Elliott introduced the Fibonacci series as:

1, 1, 2, 3, 5, 8, 13, 21, 54, 89, 144, . . .

saying, "This series is very useful in identifying and measuring every wave and the extent of each movement, and when used in conjunction with the Wave Principle is also useful in forecasting the duration of trends in various periods of time, days, weeks, months, or years. The time element as an independent device, however, continues to be baffling when attempts are made to apply any known rule of sequence to trend duration" (Elliott, p. 180).

Elliott used the Fibonacci sequence as a timing device as follows: If a trend lasted one day more than a number in the sequence, the trend must then last until the next higher number. For example, if a trend continued for 4 days, it must then last at least 5 days; if it lasted 9 days, it must then continue for at least 13 days.

Elliott had problems making this rule work, because the numbers in the sequence are too static. However, working with the ratio 1.618 in combination with peaks and valleys is very different from Elliott's time analysis. It makes the application dynamic.

Contrary to Elliott, instead of using the specific numbers in the summation series (e.g., 3, 5, 8, . . .) for time analysis, the ratio 1.618 and the reverse ratio 0.618 will be used. We will show that the ratio 1.618 can be used independently, that is, without the wave count to make time analysis possible.

TIME GOAL DAYS

Time goal days are those days in the future upon which a price event will occur. To be able to anticipate a day on which prices will achieve an objective, or reverse direction, would be a step forward in forecasting.

To calculate time goal days, we draw upon the work of the Greek mathematician Euclid, who solved the problem of relating the Golden Section to a straight line. (See Appendix A.) In Figure 1–4, the line *AB* of length *L* is divided into two segments by point *C*. Let the lengths of *AC* and *CB* be *a* and *b*, respectively. If *C* is a point such that $L:a = a:b$, then *C* is the Golden Section *AB*. The ratio $L:a$ or $a:b$ is called the *Golden ratio*. In other words, point *C* divides the line *AB* into two parts in such a way that the ratios of those parts is 1.618 and 0.618.

Our time analysis is based on the findings of Euclid. If there is one way to link Nature's Law, expressed through the Fibonacci ratio 1.618, with market swings, then it should be the way it is described in Figure 7–1.

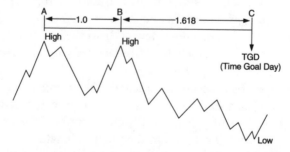

Figure 7–1   Calculation of a time goal day by using the distance between point A and B and the ratio 1.618.

Look at the peaks, *A* and *B*, in Figure 7–1. Using the distance from *A* to *B* in days (any time unit can be used), multiply that distance by the Fibonacci ratio 1.618 to forecast the resulting value *C*, which occurs on day

$$B + 1.618*(B - A)$$

C is called a *time goal day*. This is the day on which the market trend is expected to change direction.

This geometric approach has the advantage of *forecasting*, rather than lagging the market; therefore, trades can be entered or exited at the time of a price change, rather than after-the-fact. In addition, this concept is dynamic, which allows it to adjust to the longer or shorter swings of the market.

When referring to the forecasting of time goals, there is no intention to indicate that the price will be high or low when the TGD is reached. It can be either one. The time goal day only forecasts a trend change (an event) at the time the goal is reached. This is shown in Figure 7–2.

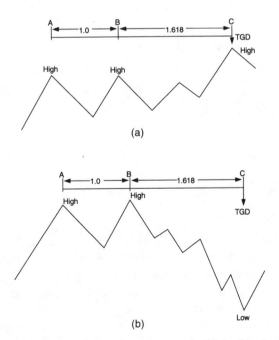

Figure 7–2 (a) At a time goal day, the price may be high; (b) at a time goal day, the price may be low.

Using Fibonacci ratios, timing of objectives can be measured on intraday, daily, weekly, or monthly charts.

TRADING USING TIME ANALYSIS

Three parts of the time analysis must work perfectly together to get the best possible results. These factors are:

- Filter size,

- Time goal days (TGDs), and

- Entry, stop-loss, and re-entry rules.

Just as with the trading signals for extensions and corrections, an investor must wait until a clear timing signal is determined before entering the market. This waiting is the toughest part of trading, for the signals always come when they are least expected. At the time of a signal, the media often recommends the opposite trade. Because this technique forecasts a change of direction, the trader must be prepared to:

- Buy when the price is low, and

- Sell when the price is high.

The following sections will answer the questions, "What is high?" and "What is low?"

What Is a Swing?

A filter *swing* is a price movement of a minimum size in one direction. Each commodity has its own special minimum criteria, or *filter*. The filter size for a commodity varies for weekly, daily, and intraday charts. It does not change once it is identified.

It will be seen later that the number of trades generated using this technique is directly proportional to the filter size. If the filter swing is *too small,* there are too many signals and frequent whipsaw losses in sideways markets. If the minimum swing size is *too large,* there are very few signals and some important trend moves are likely to be missed.

Once the correct filter size is chosen, this method should work very well in trending markets. In sidewards markets, the whipsawing should be very limited. Examples for the minimum filter sizes for several commodities are shown below. These values were generated by hand in 1983 as part of seminar material on "The Golden Section." Current testing, as far as it was possible, shows that these minimums have not changed. If Fibonacci ratios make sense, these figures should be consistent over time.

Commodity	Time Period	Filter (in pts.)	Stop Loss
Swiss franc	daily	100	100
	weekly	400	200
Deutsche mark	daily	100	100
	weekly	400	200
Japanese yen	daily	100	100
	weekly	400	200
British pound	daily	200	200
	weekly	800	400
Heating oil	daily	200	400
Treasury bonds	daily	$1^{16}/_{32}$	1.50
	weekly	3	2.00
S&P 500	daily	400	400
	hourly	100	200
Soybeans	daily	40	30
Wheat	daily	20	25
Gold	daily	15	15
Cocoa	daily	80	200
Coffee	daily	500	300
Pork bellies	daily	200	200

Swing Highs and Lows

Once the minimum swing filter has been identified on a daily chart, the filter swing is analyzed every day using a four-step procedure as follows:

Step 1. Look for a move of the minimum swing size. If the Deutsche mark minimum move has been set at 100 points, then look for a move of 100 points from the lowest low to the highest high (see Figure 7–3).

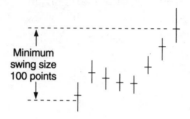

Minimum
swing size
100 points

Figure 7–3 To confirm a high or a low, we need a minimum swing size.

Step 2. The minimum swing size must be confirmed. Once the minimum swing size has been reached, the close must be higher than the high of the day which exceeded the minimum swing size (for a swing up), as shown in Figure 7–4.

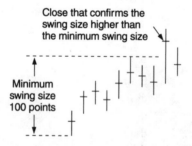

Close that confirms the
swing size higher than
the minimum swing size

Minimum
swing size
100 points

Figure 7–4 To confirm a swing size, the close has to be higher than the minimum swing size.

Step 3. On daily charts, look for a close which is lower than the low of the highest day to confirm the high day (vice versa for a low day), as shown in Figure 7–5. This step is not necessary on weekly charts because the swing size itself is bigger than on the daily charts and therefore the requirement of a confirmation would be too restrictive.

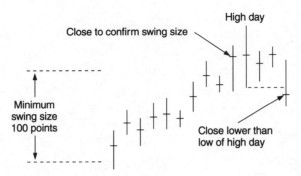

Figure 7–5 To confirm a high, the close has to be lower than the low of the highest day.

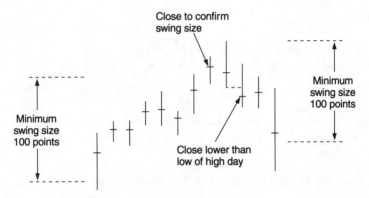

Figure 7–6 To confirm a swing high, there has to be a minimum swing size in the opposite direction from the highest high.

Step 4. Look for a minimum swing size in the opposite direction, as in Figure 7–6.

By following these four steps, the peaks and valleys are established which are needed to find the "time goal days." These four criteria may seen complicated, but they are not. The objective is to limit the number of filter swings. To do this, there must be some restrictions that reduce "noise," or there might be so many swings that we would be unable to analyze them.

Following the four-step procedure, the peaks and valleys can be marked on the daily Deutsche mark chart (Figure 7–7). Once the

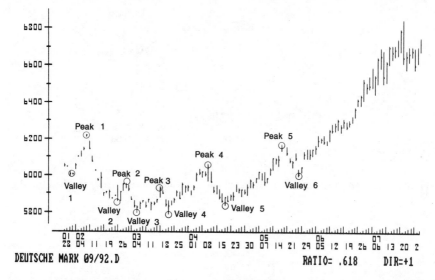

Figure 7–7   Daily Deutsche mark chart from 02-92 to 07-92. The highs and lows are marked as peak 1 to peak 5 and valley 1 to valley 6. (*Source:* TradeStation, Omega Research, Inc.)

minimum swing size is determined, the four-step procedure is the same for every product and every chart, whether weekly, daily, or intraday.

Exception: No Minimum Filter Size in a Strong Trend

Looking at the daily Deutsche mark chart, both a long sideways move and a very strong uptrend can be seen in June through July, 1992. During the strong uptrend there was no move that qualified for the new "high" or "low," based on the procedure established to identify peaks or valleys.

A standard swing high and low must occur *at least every 15 days.* If they do not occur with this frequency, the TGDs are so far apart that the market swings can no longer be captured. In addition, a lack of time goal days significantly increases trading risk. Without a nearby objective to indicate where the market will change direction, positions are held longer, and there will be larger equity swings. Computer testing shows that the best performance occurs with TGDs indicate a high or low no more than 15 days apart.

To solve this problem, whenever the market trends for at least 15 days without a minimum filter swing, we use a smaller one. We simply select the largest swing that occurred within the past 15 days,

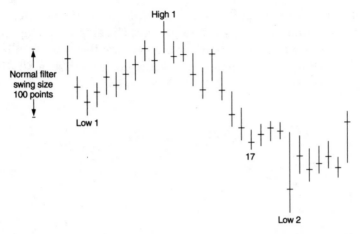

Figure 7–8 Market swing from high 1 to low 2 of 21 days without a valid swing in between.

measured from the highest high and lowest low. Figure 7–8 demonstrates this method. It is more important to maintain the frequency of TGDs than to be committed to a specific minimum swing size.

The figure shows the problem that might occur in a strongly trending market. A filter size of 100 points is assumed and shown on the left side of the chart. Low #1, high #1 and low #2 are identified.

There are 21 days between high #1 and low #2. Applying the rule for the small filter size in a trending market, look for the biggest swing between the high #1 and the low #2. That swing is located between points P1 and P2 in Figure 7–9. The new time goal day can be calculated by using the distance H1–P2, in days.

Figure 7–9 The integration of a smaller filter swing.

Returning to the daily Deutsche mark chart, the smaller swing size can be found in exactly the same way. The smaller swing high is located at peak 6 and the smaller swing low at valley 6, as seen in Figure 7–10. This is the complete procedure for establishing TGDs in strong market trends.

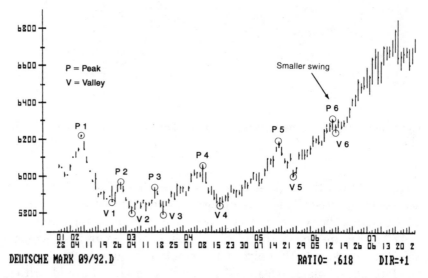

Figure 7–10 Daily Deutsche mark from 02-92 to 07-92. Smaller swing is integrated with peak 6 and valley 6. (*Source:* TradeStation, Omega Research, Inc.)

Exception: Too Many Minimum Filter Swings

The previous section redefined the minimum swing size when there were no standard swings. The opposite case also exists. Too many swings may occur in only a few days. This could easily occur in a market with slightly higher than normal volatility, as shown in Figure 7–11. Swing highs, that satisfy the minimum filter, are located at points 2, 4, and 7; swing lows are at 3 and 5.

To eliminate this excessive noise, delete the swing which has a low on the third day and the high on the fifth day, based on the following rule: *There must be at least three days between the highs and lows of two swings that satisfy the minimum swing filter.*

This applies to both top and bottom formations. Successful time analysis depends on the correct identification of peaks and valleys. The standard filter size was chosen by historical testing, but this

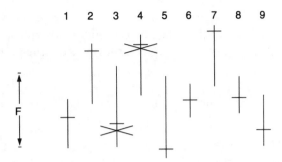

Figure 7–11   Too many minimum filter swings.

minimum filter, for example, 100 basis points in the Deutsche mark, is only the start to finding the correct peaks and valleys.

Review of the Procedure

The four-step procedure that was developed to analyze the peaks and valleys is based on a minimum swing size. This satisfies most market situations. As we have seen, there are also exceptions. In a strong bull or bear market, there are many times when a minimum swing size does not occur. Without a swing of minimum size within 15 days, the trading analysis becomes unsatisfactory. Smaller swings are integrated to solve this problem. The case with too many swings was another problem. This can happen in periods of very erratic price movement. This situation can also be solved by establishing a procedure which eliminates some of the noise.

MORE ON THE STRUCTURE OF TIME GOAL DAYS

When we look at a chart of any time span, we look at the price swings. We see big ones and small ones. These swings rarely represent the wave structure defined in the Elliott concept, because most market patterns are "irregular." As discussed earlier, those irregular market patterns are the result of complex corrections and extensions.

Working with TGDs does not require the use of a wave count. In this analysis it is not important whether there is an uptrend, downtrend, or sideways market. The Fibonacci ratio 1.618 is applied directly to well-defined market swings.

At the time the TGDs are calculated, we never know whether the market price will be high or low at the points where the TGDs are reached. It can be either one. A TGD forecast a turning point. Our objective is to:

• Sell if the market price is high when a TGD is reached, or

• Buy if the market price is low when a TGD is reached.

By using the last two highs, the TGD can be projected, as shown in the Figure 7–12.

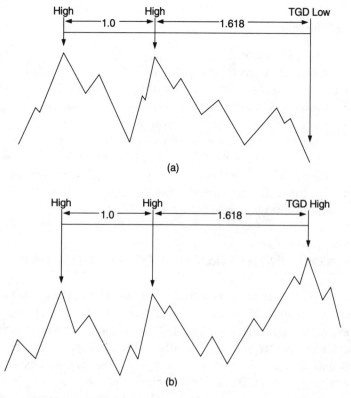

Figure 7–12 (a) Using two valid highs, the price can be low when the TGD is reached; (b) using two valid highs, the price can be high when the TGD is reached.

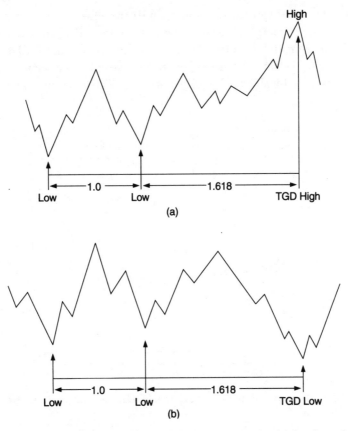

Figure 7–13   (a) Using two valid lows, the price can be high when the TGD is reached; (b) using two valid lows, the price can be low when the TGD is reached.

The same calculation performed using the two most recent highs, can be applied to the two most recent swing lows. The results are shown in Figures 7–13.

Familiarization with these four combinations will allow an understanding of what happens to the results when the TGD calculations using highs/highs and lows/lows are combined. In the best case, TGDs calculated from highs/highs or lows/lows coincide on the same day. But that is ideal. Most likely, the TGDs are interspersed. The best realistic case is when a few TGDs appear close together, forming a time band or time barrier. When multiple TGDs coincide, there is a higher probability that the market will turn for either a short-term correction or a complete trend reversal. TGDs calculated from daily data are more reliable than intraday results; weekly data takes precedence over daily data. There is less noise using longer term data.

Figure 7–14 shows the integration of TGDs using highs/highs and lows/lows.

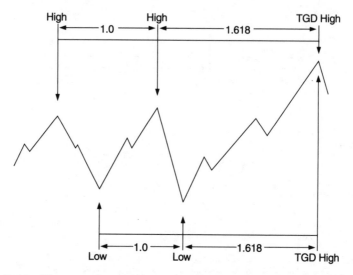

Figure 7–14   The same time targets are reached by calculating TGDs from high/high or low/low.

Problems may occur in the investment decision when the only available time-goal calculations result in TGDs which do not fall near one another. This may happen when the different time signals are based on the calculations of the last two highs and the last two lows. Figure 7–15 describes this situation.

In Figure 7–15 the time interval from *H1* to *H2* produces the time goal *H3*. The time span *L1* to *L2* gives the time goal *L3*. A short position must be entered when prices reach *H3*, because it is clearly a high price. We cannot yet know what will happen when time goal *L3* is reached, but it cannot influence the trade based on *H3*. A short is entered at *H3*, and a stop-loss is placed above the high according to the entry rule. If the position is stopped out, another short may be set at *L3* if the price is still at the same level as it was at *H3*, following the re-entry rule. If it is at a clearly low price, a new long position is entered according to the rules.

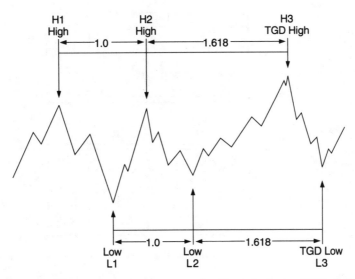

Figure 7–15   Different time targets are reached by calculating TGDs from high/high or low/low.

Analyzing Time Goal Days Based on Highs/Highs and Lows/Lows

The basic use of time goal days should be clear. In a normal market, the distance between two highs or two lows is multiplied by the ratio 1.618 to get the TGD. To start the process of working with the time goal concept, first ask the question, "Is there a filter swing high or low?" If the answer is yes, "Are we at a time goal day?"

The application of TGDs varies based on its proximity to a peak or valley. In the normal sequence of events, the market will:

- Produce a swing satisfying the minimum filter value.

- Pass a time goal day.

- Make a high or low for the current price move.

- Give an entry signal.

TGDs Occurring before or at a Peak or Valley.   In the most frequent situation, a peak or valley has not yet been seen when the TGD is reached. The location of the subsequent peak or valley is not relevant to the basic trading approach (see Figure 7–16).

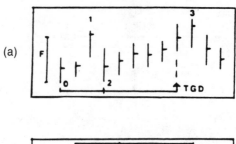

Figure 7-16 (a) TGD occurs before the peak; (b) TGD occurs at peak.

TGDs One Day after a Peak or Valley.   There are many situations where the TGD overshoots the peaks or valleys. This may go unnoticed; however, it can have made a significant change to the trade. If the TGD is one day after the peak or valley (see Figure 7–17), and on this day the entry rule still was not in effect, wait for the entry rule (entry rules are discussed later in this chapter) to enter the market.

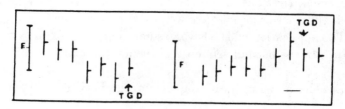

Figure 7-17   TGD occurs one day after peak.

TGDs More Than One Day after a Peak or Valley.   Whenever a TGD is more than one day after the peak or valley, the situation becomes uncertain. If no minimum swing has occurred, the TGD is ignored (see Figure 7–18).

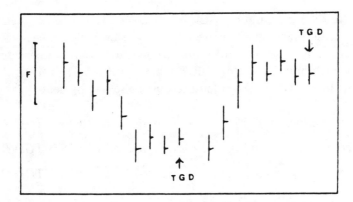

Figure 7–18   TGD occurs more than one day after peak.

Trading Example.   The four-step procedure establishes a method for identifying peaks and valleys. This procedure works for every product and every chart, whether intraday, daily or weekly. The daily Deutsche mark chart in Figure 7–19 shows the peaks and valleys that should be identified using this method.

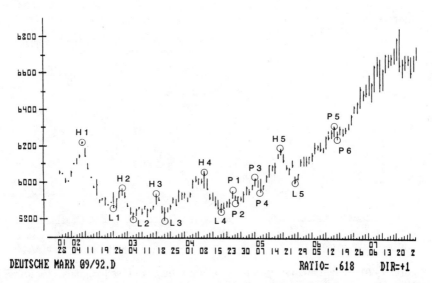

Figure 7–19   Valid peaks and valleys. (*Source:* TradeStation, Omega Research, Inc.)

With the highs and lows established, the TGDs can be calculated using the distance between the highs and the distance between the lows. For easier reference, all highs are marked even numbers and all lows with odd numbers. Only the Fibonacci ratio 1.618 was used.

The high TGDs were calculated in the following sequence:

- The distance from high #1 to high #2 times 1.618 = TGD *A*

- The distance from high #2 to high #3 times 1.618 = TGD *B*

- The distance from high #3 to high #4 times 1.618 = TGD *C*

The low TGDs were calculated in a similar sequence:

- The distance from low #1 to low #2 times 1.618 = TGD *G*

- The distance from low #2 to low #3 times 1.618 = TGD *H*

- The distance from low #3 to low #4 times 1.618 = TGD *I*

Figure 7–20 shows the peaks, valleys, and the calculated TGDs.

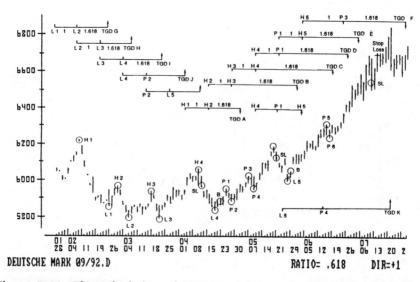

Figure 7–20 The calculation of TGDs and buy and sell signals. (*Source:* TradeStation, Omega Research, Inc.)

TGDs Using Larger Filter Swings

Larger filter swings may occur many times on weekly charts. For example, whenever there is a swing of 10 full points (1,000 basis points) in the Deutsche mark, the peaks and valleys are combined in all four ways to produce TDGs based on highs/highs, lows/lows, highs/lows, and lows/highs. The method is demonstrated in Figure 7–21, the weekly Deutsche mark chart.

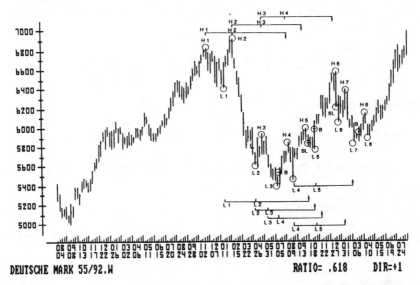

DEUTSCHE MARK 55/92.W   RATIO= .618   DIR=+1

Figure 7–21 Weekly Deutsche mark chart from 07-89 to 07-92. Buy and sell signals generated with the time analysis. (*Source:* TradeStation, Omega Research, Inc.)

REVIEW

This chapter showed how important it is to produce the TGDs which integrate with the time frame of the analysis. It also showed what happens when a TGD is reached. It confirms the power that lies in this analysis, but also demonstrated how much accuracy and discipline it takes to follow the strategy.

The occurrence of the TGD in relationship to the developing peak or valley was important. Whenever a TGD fell more than one day after a peak or valley, it was ignored, provided a minimum swing has not occurred.

In strong markets, there may be intervals of 15 days in which a swing does not satisfy the minimum filter criteria needed to calculate a TGD. In this case, a combination of the previous highs/lows or lows/highs can be used to generate the TGDs needed.

On weekly charts, there may be very large swings which produce TGDs that are months away. To solve this problem, the combination of highs/lows and lows/highs was also used. For example, a full 10-point swing (50.00–60.00) in the Deutsche mark is considered big.

ADDITIONAL RULES

Normal Entry Rule

A new short position is entered using the following steps:

- First, prices must move up by more than the minimum required swing,

- Then, a TGD is passed, and

- Last, we sell on the close when the closing price is below the low of the highest day.

This entry sequence is shown in Figure 7–22. The normal buy entry rule follows the same procedure.

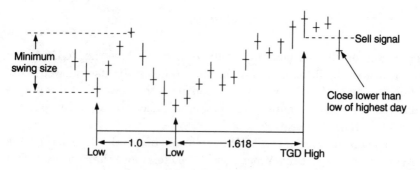

Figure 7–22   Normal entry rule.

Additional Entry Rule

An additional entry rule should give us the chance to enter the market when there is a very strong move. In this case we want to be invested before the market closes. For the additional entry rule, a sell signal is as follows (and shown in Figure 7–23):

- After the minimum swing up has been satisfied, and
- After a TGD has been passed, then
- Sell when the price breaks the previous 4 lows.

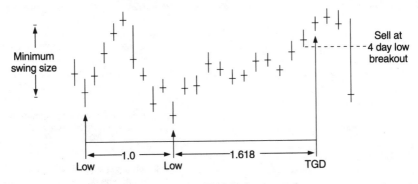

Figure 7–23   Additional entry rule.

The additional buy entry rule is:

- After the minimum swing down has been satisfied, and
- After a TGD has been passed, then
- Buy when prices break the 4 previous highs.

Stop-Loss Rule

A stop loss should always be entered at the same time as the trade entry. One effective way of placing a stop loss is to work with a price square (see Chapter 3, Figure 3–14). On the daily chart, the side of the square is the distance of five business days. On a weekly chart, the side is the distance of five weeks (see Figure 7–24).

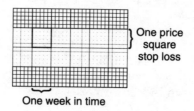

One price square stop loss

One week in time

Figure 7–24   Stop loss rule.

Re-Entry Rule

Whenever a long position is stopped out, it may be re-entered if market conditions satisfy the normal entry rule, and the market did not make an upward move satisfying the swing filter size. This can be seen in Figure 7–25.

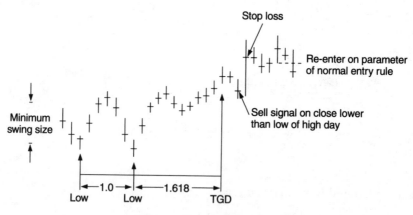

Figure 7–25   Re-entry rule.

Whenever a short position is stopped out, a re-entry occurs when market conditions satisfy the normal entry rule, and the market did not make a downward move satisfying the swing filter size.

SUMMARY

Elliott wrote of timing, "The length of waves may vary, but not the number of waves. The numbers of this series [Fibonacci sequence] are useful in timing the waves, both advancing and declining" (p. 129).

A move that extends itself beyond three days should not reverse until *five* days are reached. A move that exceeds *five* days should last *eight* days. A trend of *nine* days should not finish before *thirteen* days, and so on. This basic structure of calculating trend changes is the same for hourly, daily, weekly, and monthly data. Each one of these cases is an example of the Fibonacci ratio, and the basis for time goal days.

Our approach to timing is focused only on the Fibonacci ratio 1.618. It is very mechanical and seems to work in both sideways and trending markets. While Elliott's approach is very static, our analysis is very dynamic.

The greatest difference between this and strategies introduced previously, is that in this concept we are invested most of the time.

This concept is closely related to Nature's Law, expressed through the Fibonacci ratio 1.618. This means the TGD concept has forecasting value; it anticipates price changes rather than following after them. This distinguishes it from many other trading methods. The unique combination of swing size, time goal days, and entry rules makes it possible to pinpoint tops and bottoms. In addition, this concept is dynamic, allowing it to adjust to bigger and smaller market moves.

8

COMBINING PRICE AND TIME

This chapter analyzes whether signals, based on a combination of price and time, will make trading safer and more profitable. "Timing is the most essential element. What to buy is important, when to buy is more important. Investment markets progressively foretell their own future. Observation of waves indicate the next movement of the market by their patterns whose beginning and ending are susceptible to definite and conclusive analysis" (Elliott, p. 84). As mentioned before, there does not seem to be any evidence that Elliott provided mechanical rules to forecast price moves as part of his concept. But by focusing on the Fibonacci ratio 1.618, it is possible to calculate and forecast price and time goals. Now we will combine them into one analysis.

For the purposes of demonstration, weekly charts will be used. The same principle can be applied to both daily and intraday data.

CONCEPT OF COMBINING PRICE AND TIME

Step 1. The Correction

In this method, wave count is disregarded. If there is a minimum swing of, for example, 10 points (60.00–70.00) in the Deutsch mark

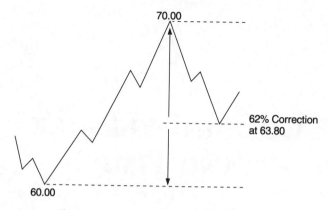

Figure 8–1   62% correction price target.

(see Figure 8–1), wait for a correction of at least 62% of the total amplitude of the previous swing from point *A* to *B*. This technique was described in detail in Chapter 4.

Step 2. The Extension

Extensions were described in detail in a previous chapter. An extension can be measured in the direction of the main trend by multiplying the total amplitude of wave 1 by 1.618 as shown in Figure 8–2 (the minimum swing size is required); or, as part of the correction by multiplying the total amplitude of wave *a* by 1.618, as in Figure 8–3.

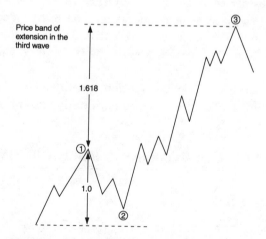

Figure 8–2   The end of an extension calculated by using the ratio 1.618.

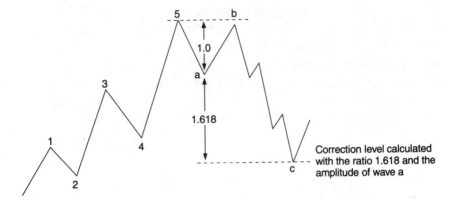

Figure 8–3 The end of a correction using the ratio 1.618 and the amplitude of wave a of the correction.

Step 3. Timing

To calculate time, identify two peaks or valleys and multiply the distance between the two by the ratio 1.618. This step is described in completely in Chapter 7. An example of a TGD based on two valleys is shown in Figure 8–4.

The result of combining the price goals and time goals calculated with Fibonacci ratio 1.618 are target points where both strategies coincide.

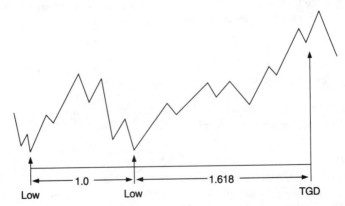

Figure 8–4 The calculation of a time goal day using two valleys and the ratio 1.618.

A BRITISH POUND EXAMPLE

The British pound weekly chart will be used as an example of combining price and time. In this example there are five major trend changes marked at points *A, B, C, D,* and *E* indicated in Figure 8–5. This chart also shows the buy and sell signals generated from the rules using extensions and corrections in previous chapters.

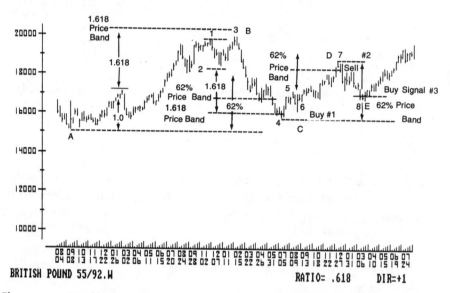

BRITISH POUND 55/92.W **RATIO= .618** **DIR=+1**

Figure 8–5 Weekly British pound chart from 08-89 to 07-92. Buy and sell signals using price targets calculated with 62% corrections and extensions using the ratio 1.618. (*Source:* TradeStation, Omega Research, Inc.)

Trading Signals Based on Extensions and Corrections

Using the price goals calculated from extensions and corrections, the following trading procedure will occur.

Buy Signal at Point C. The swing from point *A* to point *B* was followed by a correction of more than 62%. There was also an extension of 1.618 times the amplitude of the swing from point #1 to point #2. Price dropped lower than the 62% correction and turned exactly at the price goal precalculated for the extension. A long position was set following the entry rule after the trend change at point Buy #1.

Sell Signal after Point D. There was a 62% correction of the swing from point *B* to point *C;* however, the price target for the extension was not reached. A sell signal was generated after the trend changed at sell point #2.

Buy Signal after Point E. There was another 62% correction of the swing from point *C* to point *D.* A buy signal occurred after the trend changed at point *E* in point #3.

Trading Signals Based on Time Analysis

The same weekly British pound chart (Figure 8–5) will now be used to demonstrate buy and sell signals based on time analysis. In these examples, different numbers are used to mark peaks and valleys.

Sell Signal after Peak #4. The swing from low #3 to high #4 fulfills the minimum filter requirement. The distance form low #1 to low #2 multiplied by 1.618 gives the time goal day before peak #4. Sell signal #1 occurred on the close below the low of the highest day.

Sell Signal after Peak #6. A very large swing is formed form low #5 to high #6. Apply one of the exceptions, for weekly charts, by multiplying the distance from high #4 to low #5 by 1.618 to get the time goal day before peak #6.

Sell Signal after Peak #8. Another big swing formed by the move from low #7 to high #8, causing another exception for the weekly chart. Multiply the distance from high #6 to low #7 by 1.618 to get the time goal day before peak #8. Sell signal #3 appears on the close below the low of the highest day.

The trades shown in Figure 8–6 were all generated in the sequence given for *sell signal #1.* The time goal days which preceded the signals can be easily identified.

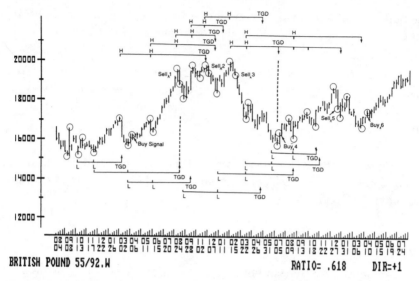

BRITISH POUND 55/92.W   **RATIO= .618   DIR=+1**

Figure 8–6   Weekly British pound chart from 08-89 to 07-92. Buy and sell signals using the time analysis with time goals days and entry rules. (*Source:* TradeStation, Omega Research, Inc.)

SUMMARY

If we compare the signals in Figure 8–5 generated by price with those in Figure 8–6 which were the produce of time, it can be said:

- There is no particular order in the signals. Trades resulting from extensions can occur before or after those based on corrections.

- The technique of working with time goal days is very different from that of using extensions or corrections. By using time goal days, we hold a market position most of the time. Because the objective is to stay close to the trend, the result is that there are more trades in sideways periods than in trending markets.

- The time goal signals, and signals based on 62% corrections, coincided with all major trend changes within the test period. Although this feature was not used in the trading strategy, if offers interesting possibilities for improving performance.

9

THE LOGARITHMIC SPIRAL

The *logarithmic spiral* provides the link between price and time analysis. It is the answer to a long search for a solution to forecasting both price and time. The logarithmic spiral is called the most beautiful of mathematical curves. It was briefly discussed in Chapter 1. This spiral has occurred for millions of years in nature. It is the only mathematical curve to follow the pattern of growth expressed in the spira mirabilis, commonly called the nautilus shell. Two segments of the spiral may be different in size but not in shape. The spiral is without a terminal point. Figure 9–1 shows that, as the size of the chambers increase in the proportion of the Fibonacci ratio 1.618, its shape remains unchanged.

Figure 9–1   Logarithmic spiral shown in the nautilus shell.

If there is any chance of linking human behavior, expressed in the price swings of stocks and commodities, with Nature's Law expressed in the nautilus shell, the logarithmic spiral should be the closest solution. Any point on the spiral represents the optimum price-time relationship.

The most challenging part of the spiral is to see it work in extreme market situations, when behavioral patterns are strongest. The stock market crash in October 1987 is such an example. While every other method of analysis seems to fail, the correct spiral isolates the bottom of the move precisely (see Figure 9–2).

With the center of the spiral at point B and the starting point at A, the spiral was penetrated by the S&P price at point C. It will be shown later that points A and B are very definitive and could have been selected by any investor using the rules explained in this chapter.

THE CONCEPT OF THE SPIRAL

The spiral is easy to understand and conceptually simple to apply to the markets. But, because it identifies turning points, the trading signals

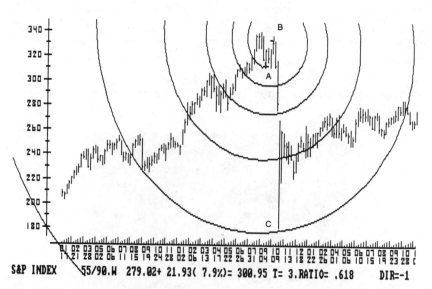

S&P INDEX   55/90.W 279.02+ 21.93(7.9%)= 300.95 T= 3.RATIO= .618   DIR=-1

Figure 9–2 Weekly S&P chart from 01-86 to 11-88. The price target was reached at point C with center of the spiral at point B and the starting point at point A. (*Source:* Robert Fischer Research, Chicago.)

require that positions be taken counter to the current price trend (i.e., selling when the price is high); that requires exceptional discipline on the part of the trader to execute the signals. But it can be proved that, with the correct center chosen, the spiral can identify turning points in the markets with an accuracy never seen before. This is not a black box approach, nor an overfitted computerized system, but a universal law applied to commodity price movement.

Market Symmetry

The logarithmic spiral shows that there is a stunning symmetry in the price pattern of commodity charts. The existence of this symmetry proves that market moves are not random, but follow a clear behavioral pattern. These forces which direct the price moves also allow the investor the opportunity to profit. It is only necessary to turn these principles into trading rules. The weekly crude oil chart (see Figure 9–3) is another example of the remarkable timing possible using the spiral.

By placing the center of the spiral at point A and the starting point at B, the spiral went precisely through the lows at point C and point D, and also touched the highs at points E and F.

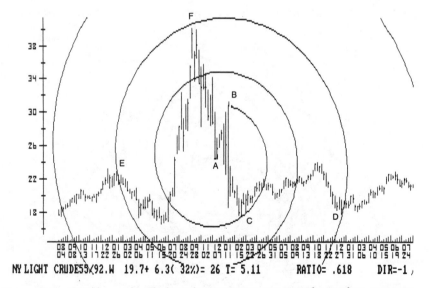

NY LIGHT CRUDE55X92.W 19.7+ 6.3(32%)= 26 T= 5.11   RATIO= .618   DIR=-1 ⁄

Figure 9–3 Weekly crude oil chart from 07-89 to 06-92. The perfect symmetry in the market is shown with the center of the spiral at point A and the starting point at point B. (*Source:* Robert Fischer Research, Chicago.)

Using the weekly crude oil chart as an example, the symmetry of any chart can be found once the correct center of the spiral is identified. This center can be either in the middle of the market pattern or at one of the extreme points (highs or lows). The use of either daily or weekly charts does not affect the accuracy of the spiral. It is just as likely that this same principle will work on intraday charts; however, the increase in noise makes the center of the spiral more difficult to locate, and the profit margins tend to become very narrow.

Rule of Alternation

The *rule of alternation* is the second important rule (after the Fibonacci ratio) which shows that Nature's Law can be applied to price patterns in commodities. This law is best described by the example of a sunflower as given by Jay Hambidge, "In the sunflower two sets of equiangular spirals are superimposed or intertwined, one being right handed and the other a left handed spiral, with each floret filling a dual role by belonging to both spirals" (*Practical Applications of Dynamic Symmetry*, Jay Hambidge, New York: Dover Publications, 1970, pp. 28, 29). This formation is shown in Figure 9–4.

Elliott knew about the rule of alternation. This rule made it possible for him to claim that he could forecast future price moves based

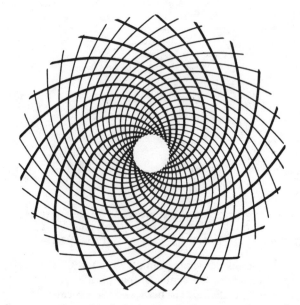

Figure 9–4   The rule of alternation is shown on the sunflower.

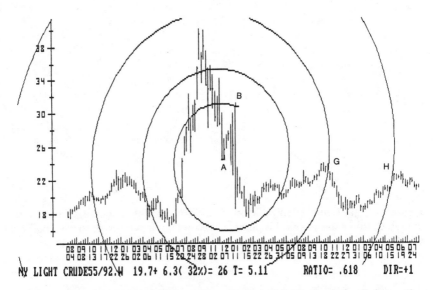

NY LIGHT CRUDE55/92.W   19.7+ 6.3(32%)= 26 T= 5.11   RATIO= .618   DIR=+1

Figure 9–5   Weekly crude oil chart from 07-89 to 06-92. The rule of alternation can be seen by turning the spiral counterclockwise instead of clockwise in Figure 9–3. (*Source:* Robert Fischer Research, Chicago.)

on the formation in wave 2 and wave 4 (*The Wave Principle,* Elliott, p. 51). This was described in detail in Chapter 2.

Figure 9–5 shows how the rule of alternation can be applied strictly to the spiral. In the previous example, using the weekly crude oil chart, perfect symmetry was found by turning the spiral clockwise. In Figure 9–3 the spiral pinpointed the lows at *C* and *D*. Starting at the same center point *A* and the same starting point *B*, but turning the spiral counterclockwise, Figure 9–5 isolates the exact highs at points *G* and *H*.

Does this mean that the spiral is the perfect forecasting instrument, and that the rule of alternation will tell us when there is a high and a low? Maybe! But the rule of alternation must still pass the final test. The reason for the hesitation is that, after identifying a low with a spiral that runs clockwise, the spiral counterclockwise might identify either:

• The turning point as a high as shown in Figure 9–6a, or

• The turning point as an even lower low, shown in Figure 9–6b.

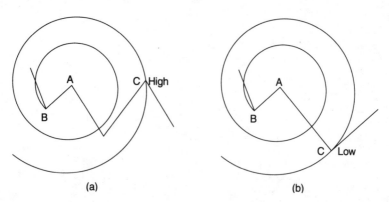

(a)   (b)

Figure 9–6 **(a) Center of spiral in point A, starting point at point B, turning point at high C; (b) center of spiral is point A, starting point at point B, turning point at low C.**

MORE ON THE STRUCTURE OF THE SPIRAL

This is not the first time that the spiral has been used to solve a business problem. It has long been used in industrial engineering. But this is the first time, as far as we know, that this instrument has been used to analyze price data in stocks and commodities.

We developed a computer program to automatically plot the spiral according to the rules of nature. The spiral never changes its shape. It grows from the center in the Fibonacci ratio 1.618. The formula for the logarithmic spiral is:

$$\text{Cot } \alpha = 2/\pi \times \ln\varphi$$

More details about the mathematical application of the spiral can be found in *The Divine Proportion,* by H.E. Huntley, page 172 ff.

Because the intention of this book is educational, the formula for the spiral is presented for those interested readers. In addition, Appendix B contains a computer printout of the *BASIC* program source code for producing the logarithmic spiral given the focus and starting point. Readers may use this code as a basis for their own programs. More tools should follow in the future.

The size of the spiral is determined by the distance between the center and the starting point. Every time the spiral makes a full turn it extends itself by the Fibonacci ratio 1.618. In Figure 9–7, the weekly chart of the Japanese yen:

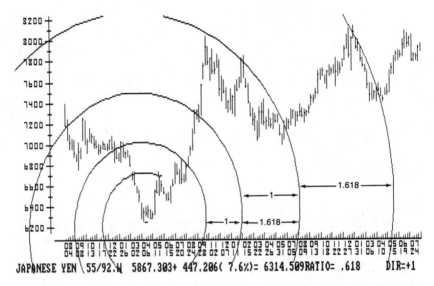

Figure 9–7 Weekly Japanese yen chart from 07-89 to 07-92. The spiral grows by the ratio 1.618 which is every time it completes a full cycle. (*Source:* Robert Fischer Research, Chicago.)

- The center of the spiral is at point *A*,
- The starting point is at *B*,
- After the first full rotation has been completed, at point *C*, the spiral has expanded by 0.618 times the distance from *A* to *B*, and
- After the second full cycle, at point *E*, it has grown by 1.618 times the distance from *A* to *B* and 1.618 times the distance from *B* to *C*.

This growth pattern does not change as the spiral extends itself.

Deciding Which Way to Rotate the Spiral

The rule of alternation shows that the spiral could be turned either clockwise (Figure 9–8a) or counterclockwise (Figure 9–8b), beginning from the same center and starting points. Research also shows that, in order to catch every turning point, it is necessary to work with both possibilities. This is also essential if the rule of alternation is to be integrated into the strategy. For those who choose to limit the combinations, the best results will be found by concentrating on the spiral that turns counterclockwise.

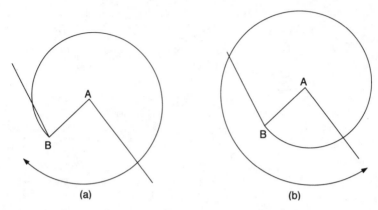

Figure 9–8 (a) Spiral turns clockwise, center at point A, starting point at point B; (b) spiral turns counterclockwise, center at point A, starting point at point B.

Swing Size

The swing size determines the size of the spiral. A minimum swing size is needed for practical purposes. To find the best swing size on a daily or weekly chart is very mechanical and should not present a problem to non-mathematical users. The result of choosing the wrong swing size is readily apparent:

- If the swing size is too small, there is too much noise, causing the swings to be unreliable; and, the corrections do not offer enough profit potential.

- If the swing size is too big, the spiral rings are too far away and are then of no value.

As a guideline, Table 9–1 illustrates some of the swing sizes that will be useful to the reader.

To confirm a swing high or low, the following procedure is necessary:

Step 1. When looking for a high, find the swing size measured from the lowest low to the highest high, but not less than minimum value given in Table 9–1 (the opposite for a low).

Table 9–1

Commodity	Daily	Weekly
	(In full points)	
S&P 500	4.00	8.00
Treasury bonds	2.00	4.00
Crude oil	2.00	3.00
Soybeans	10.00	20.00
Pork bellies	2.00	4.00
Swiss franc	2.00	4.00
Deutsche mark	2.00	4.00
Japanese yen	2.00	4.00
British pound	3.00	6.00

Step 2. To confirm the swing high using daily charts (*not* weekly), find a close that is lower than the low of the day on which the high occurred.

Step 3. There has to be at least a 38% downward correction following the highest high (the opposite for a low).

Figure 9–9 shows this sequence of steps for the confirmation of a high.

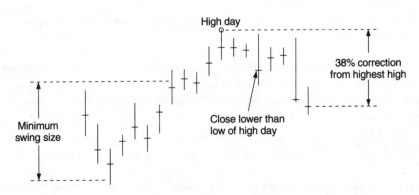

Figure 9–9 The sequence of steps for the confirmation of a high.

Specifying the Spiral

Center of the Spiral. Finding the center of the spiral and the correct starting point is the most critical part of the analysis. There is no doubt that every top or bottom can be pinpointed if the correct spiral is chosen.

To find the center of the spiral, look at the three waves normally seen at bigger trend changes. This 3-swing pattern, also known as an *a-b-c* correction, seems to include everything needed to forecast the next turning point in the market. Figure 9–10 shows the possible combinations of the 3-swing pattern that can be used to draw the spirals on any daily or weekly chart.

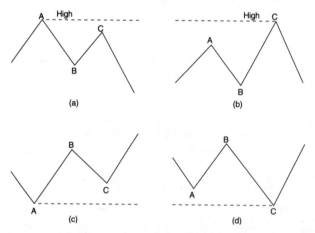

Figure 9–10 (a) 3-swing pattern in a downswing. Point A is the highest high; (b) 3-swing pattern in a downtrend. Point C is the highest high; (c) 3-swing pattern in an upswing. Point A is the lowest low; (d) 3-swing pattern in an upswing. Point C is the lowest low.

When the 3-swing pattern is used, we have the option of locating the center of the spiral at point *A, B,* or *C.* But the 3-swing pattern used to draw the spiral remains the same whether an uptrend or downtrend is being identified. Because the entire concept is difficult to visualize, the starting points for the uptrend and downtrend will be shown separately, even though they are identical, only reversed.

Starting Points for the Spiral in a Downtrend. Because a spiral can be drawn from any of the three center points *A, B,* or *C,* using either of the remaining points as the starting location, there are:

- 4 options for drawing the spiral clockwise, and

- 4 options for drawing the spiral counterclockwise.

These eight combinations are shown in Figure 9–11. Although the eight formations would catch every top and bottom, the best overall results are achieved by using point B as the center. For the sake of simplicity, the following combination will be used:

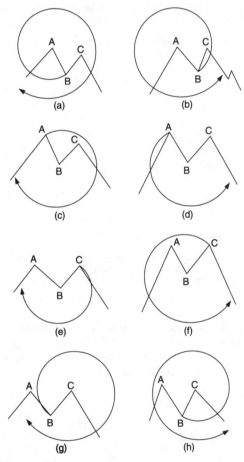

Figure 9–11 Possible combinations of 3-swing pattern in a downtrend with the center in point A-B-C and the starting points in point A-B-C. (a) Spiral clockwise center at A, start at B; (b) spiral counterclockwise start at B, center at A; (c) spiral clockwise center at B, start at A; (d) spiral counterclockwise center at B, start at A; (e) spiral clockwise center at B, start at C; (f) spiral counterclockwise center at B, start at C; (g) spiral clockwise center at C, start at B; (h) spiral counterclockwise center at C, start at B.

- The center of the spiral will be point *B*,

- The starting point will be either *A* or *C*, and

- The spiral will turn either clockwise or counterclockwise.

These options are shown in the following four cases:

Case 1. In the weekly pork belly chart the center of the spiral is at point *B*, and the starting point is *A*. The spiral is turned clockwise. The direction of the trend changed when the price penetrated the spiral at point *D*. This can be seen in Figure 9–12.

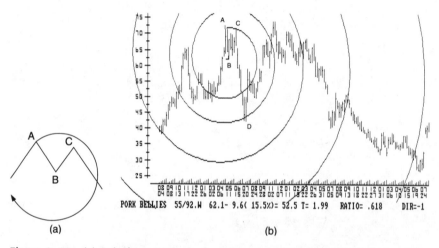

(a)   (b)

Figure 9–12 (a) Spiral turns clockwise with center at point B and the starting point at point A. (b) weekly pork belly chart from 07-89 to 07-92. Spiral turns clockwise, center at point B, start at point A, price target at point D. (*Source:* Robert Fischer Research, Chicago.)

Case 2. In the daily soybean chart the center of the spiral is at *B*, and the starting point at *A*. The spiral is turned counterclockwise. The trend changed when the price penetrated the spiral at *D*. This is shown in Figure 9–13.

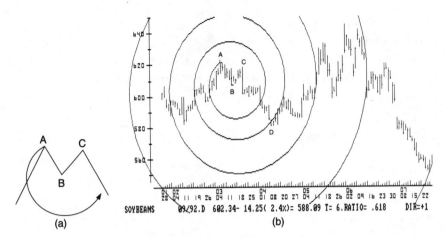

SOYBEANS   09/92.D   602.34- 14.25(2.4%)= 588.09 T= 6.RATIO= .618   DIR=+1

(a)   (b)

Figure 9–13   (a) Spiral turns counterclockwise, start at point A, center at point B; (b) daily soybean chart from 01-92 to 07-92. Spiral turns counterclockwise, center at point B, start at point A, price target at point D. (*Source:* Robert Fischer Research, Chicago.)

Case 3.   In the daily Swiss franc chart the center of the spiral is at *B*, and the starting point is at *C*. The spiral turns clockwise. The trend changed when the price penetrated the spiral at point *D*. This is shown in Figure 9–14.

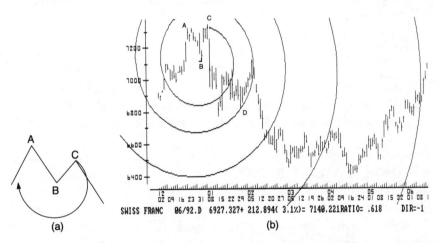

SWISS FRANC   06/92.D   6927.327+ 212.894(3.1%)= 7140.221RATIO= .618   DIR=-1

(a)   (b)

Figure 9–14   (a) Spiral turns clockwise, center at point B, start at point C; (b) daily Swiss franc chart from 12-91 to 06-92. Spiral turns clockwise, center at point B, start at point C, price target at point D. (*Source:* Robert Fischer Research, Chicago.)

Case 4. In the weekly Swiss franc chart the center of the spiral is at point *B*, and the starting point is *C*. The spiral is turned counterclockwise. The direction of the trend changed when the price penetrated the spiral at point *D*. This is shown in Figure 9–15.

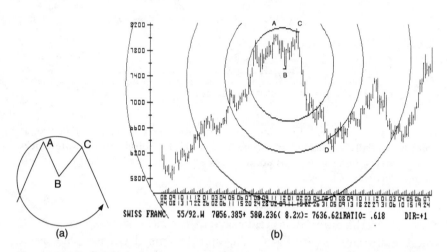

SWISS FRANC 55/92.W 7056.385+ 580.236(8.2%)= 7636.621RATIO= .618   DIR=+1

(a)   (b)

Figure 9–15 (a) Spiral turns counterclockwise, center at point B, start at point C; (b) weekly Swiss franc chart from 07-89 to 07-92. Spiral turns counterclockwise, center at point B, starting point at point C, price target at point D. (*Source:* Robert Fischer Research, Chicago.)

Although years of study show that turning the spiral counterclockwise gives better overall results than turning it clockwise, both options are still necessary to satisfy the rule of alternation.

Starting Points for the Spirals in an Uptrend. The spiral centers chosen from the three points *A*, *B*, and *C* have the same options shown for the downtrend, only in reverse. In total, there are four options to turn the spiral clockwise, and four options to turn the spiral counterclockwise. These options are shown in Figure 9–16a-h. As with the downtrend, it is possible to use all eight options to find every top and bottom, but the best results were achieved by using the center at point *B*. Therefore, examples will be limited to:

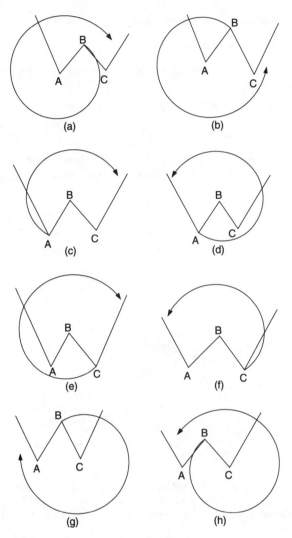

Figure 9–16 Eight options in an uptrend to turn the spiral clockwise or counter-clockwise with different centers and starting points. (a) Spiral turns clockwise, center at A, start at B; (b) spiral turns counterclockwise, center at A, start at B; (c) spiral turns clockwise, center at B, start at A; (d) spiral turns counterclock-wise, center at B, start at A; (e) spiral turns clockwise, center at B, start at C; (f) spiral turns counterclockwise, start at C, center at B; (g) spiral turns clockwise, center at C, start at B; (h) spiral turns counterclockwise, center at C, start at B.

- The center of the spiral at point *B*,
- The starting point at either *A* or *C*, and
- Turning the spiral either clockwise or counterclockwise.

These four options are shown in the following examples:

Case 1.   In the daily soybean chart the center of the spiral is at point *B*, and the starting point is at *A*. The spiral turns clockwise. The trend changed when the price penetrated the spiral at point *D*, as seen in Figure 9–17.

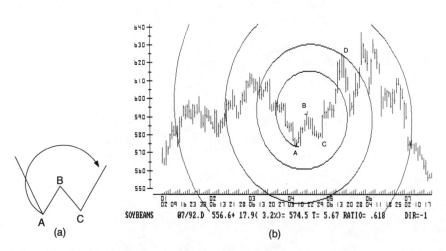

Figure 9–17   (a) Spiral turns clockwise, center at point B, start at point A; (b) daily soybean chart from 01-92 to 07-92. Spiral turns clockwise, center at point B, starting point at point A, price target at point D. (*Source:* Robert Fischer Research, Chicago.)

Case 2.   In the weekly British pound chart the center of the spiral is at *B*, and the starting point at *A*. The spiral is turned counterclockwise. The trend changed when the price penetrated the spiral at point *D*. This is shown in Figure 9–18.

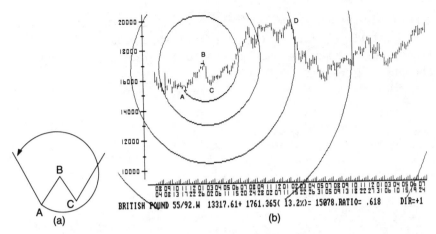

Figure 9–18 (a) Spiral turns counterclockwise, center at point B, start at point A; (b) weekly British pound chart, spiral turns counterclockwise, center at point B, starting point at point A, price target at point D. (*Source:* Robert Fischer Research, Chicago.)

Case 3. In the weekly Treasury bond chart the center of the spiral is at *B*, and the starting point is at *C*. The spiral turns clockwise. The direction of the trend changed when the price penetrated the spiral at point *D*. This is shown in Figure 9–19.

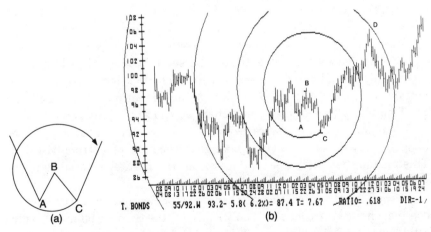

Figure 9–19 (a) Spiral turns clockwise, center at point B, starting point at point C; (b) weekly TSY-bond chart from 07-89 to 07-92. Spiral turns clockwise, center at point B, starting point at point C, price target at point D. (*Source:* Robert Fischer Research, Chicago.)

Case 4. In the weekly crude oil chart the center of the spiral is at *B*, and the starting point is at *C*. The spiral turns counterclockwise. The trend changed when the price penetrated the spiral at point *D*. This is shown in Figure 9–20.

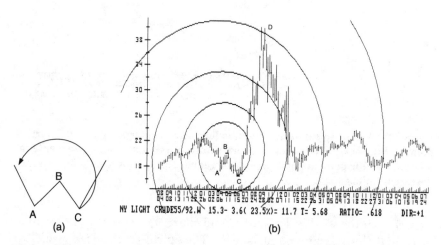

Figure 9–20 (a) Spiral turns counterclockwise, center at point B, starting point at point C; (b) weekly crude oil chart from 07-89 to 07-92. Spiral turns counterclockwise, center at point B, starting point at point C, price target at point D. (*Source:* Robert Fischer Research, Chicago.)

All the cases are conceptually the same because they have a 3-swing pattern. Chapter 4 described the identification of the 3-swing pattern as part of the Elliott findings on corrections. These swings can frequently be found at trend changes and are highly reliable.

The spiral cannot be drawn without a 3-swing pattern, which happens only if there is a trend change in the form of a strong *V*-turn. This means that after a strong upswing, the market reverses with a very strong downswing and no correction.

Applying the spiral to any other wave, for example wave 3 or wave 4, does not change the concept. It only confirms the turning points already established by another spiral. To keep the picture complete, Figures 9–21 and 9–22 show spirals drawn from wave 3 and wave 4, respectively.

On the daily Swiss franc chart (Figure 9–21) the center of the spiral is at point *A*. The starting point is point *B* at the end of wave 3.

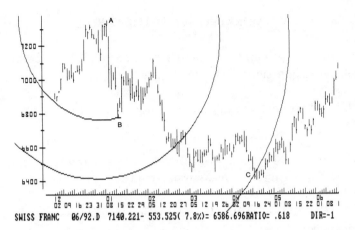

SWISS FRANC   06/92.D 7140.221- 553.525(7.8%)= 6586.696RATIO= .618   DIR=-1

Figure 9–21 Daily Swiss franc chart from 12-91 to 06-92. Spiral turns clock-wise, center at point A, starting point at point B, price target at point C. (*Source:* Robert Fischer Research, Chicago.)

The trend direction changes when the price penetrates the spiral at point C. In this case, only the swing size from *A* to *B* is used.

On the weekly crude oil chart (Figure 9–22) the center of the spiral is at *A*. The starting point is *B* at the end of wave 4. The spiral is turned counterclockwise. The trend changed when the spiral was penetrated at point C.

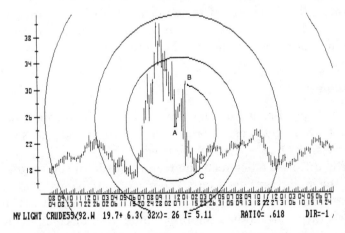

NY LIGHT CRUDE55X92.W 19.7+ 6.3(32%)= 26 I= 5.11   RATIO= .618   DIR=-1

Figure 9–22 Weekly crude oil chart from 07-89 to 07-92, Spiral turns counter-clockwise, center at point A, starting point at point B, price target at point C. (*Source:* Robert Fischer Research, Chicago.)

WORKING WITH THE SPIRAL

Each time we begin an analysis using the spiral, it is necessary to ask the following questions:

Step 1. Is there a 3-swing pattern that satisfies the minimum swing size?

Step 2. Have there been two full rotations around the center of the spiral, and has ring 2, as measured from the center, been penetrated?

Step 3. Has the entry rule been satisfied (as discussed in Chapter 6, "Extensions of Wave 3")?

All three steps must be answered "Yes" to have a valid spiral signal. The analysis of spirals offers the option of choosing between different spiral rings. Even when the correct center and starting point is known, it is also necessary to know at which spiral ring the market will turn. The following sections discuss the different spiral rings.

Spiral Ring 1

At this time no rules have been offered for investing when spiral ring 1 is penetrated. Ring 1 can be of some importance when working with big swing sizes. It cannot be used with small swings, because it can often be confused with noise and therefore lacks reliability.

Spiral Ring 2

The use of spiral ring 2 overlaps the analysis of extensions described in Chapter 6. In both cases the same minimum swing size is used, and the same entry and exit rules are used.

The difference between the techniques is in the target points, where the signal entries occur. The use of extensions limits entries to price targets based only on the Fibonacci ratio 1.618. The spiral locates a target which is a combination of both price and time. This adds another dimension to the analysis, and makes it even more unique. When the correct spiral is chosen, the results are much more precise.

To become more familiar with the spiral analysis, Figure 9–23 shows three consecutive signals in the same weekly pork belly chart. In all three cases:

- There is a 3-swing pattern,
- Spiral ring 2 is penetrated, and
- The entry rule in Chapter 6, "Extension of Wave 3," case 1, is used.

Case 1. In this weekly pork belly chart the 3-swing pattern was marked *A*, *B*, and *C*. The center of the spiral is at point *B*. The starting point is at *C*. The spiral turns counterclockwise. Once ring 2 of the spiral is penetrated at point *D*, we look for the entry rule to be satisfied. A sell signal occurs when the 2-week low is penetrated.

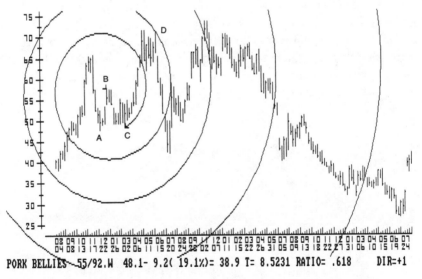

PORK BELLIES--55/92.W   48.1- 9.2(19.1%)= 38.9 T= 8.5231 RATIO= .618   DIR=+1

Figure 9–23   Weekly pork bellies chart from 08-89 to 07-92. Spiral turns counterclockwise, center at point B, starting point at point C, price target at point D. (*Source:* Robert Fischer Research, Chicago.)

Case 2. Using the same weekly pork belly chart there is a second 3-swing pattern marked with the points *A, B,* and *C.* The center of the spiral is at point *B.* The starting point is at *A.* The spiral turns counterclockwise. The trend changed when the price penetrated the spiral at point *D.* A long position is entered when the 2-week high is penetrated, as shown in Figure 9–24.

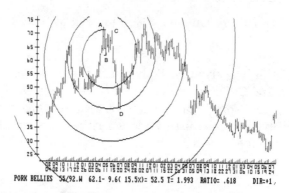

PORK BELLIES 55/92.W 62.1- 9.6(15.5%)= 52.5 T= 1.993 RATIO= .618 DIR=+1

Figure 9–24 Weekly pork bellies chart from 08-89 to 07-92. Spiral turns counterclockwise, center at point B, starting point at point A, price target at point D. (*Source:* Robert Fischer Research, Chicago.)

Case 3. Again, the weekly pork belly chart shows a third 3-swing pattern marked with points *A, B,* and *C* (see Figure 9–25). The center of the spiral is at point *C.* The starting point is at *B.* The spiral turns counterclockwise. The trend changed when the price penetrated ring 2 of the spiral at point *D.* A short position is set when the previous 2-week low is penetrated.

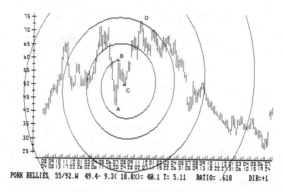

PORK BELLIES 55/92.W 49.4- 9.3(18.8%)= 40.1 T= 5.11 RATIO= .618 DIR=+1

Figure 9–25 Weekly pork bellies chart from 08-89 to 07-92. Spiral turns counterclockwise, center at point C, starting point at point B, price target at point D. (*Source:* Robert Fischer Research, Chicago.)

After three cases exemplifying how the spiral works on a weekly pork belly chart, it is still necessary to give examples of different products in order to show that the spiral is not limited to special products or time frames. On the daily S&P 500 (Figure 9–26) there is a 3-swing pattern indicated by points *A*, *B*, and *C*. The center of the spiral is at point *A;* the starting point is *B*. The spiral turns clockwise. The trend changed when the S&P price penetrated ring 2 of the spiral at point *D*. A long position is set when the previous 2-day high was broken.

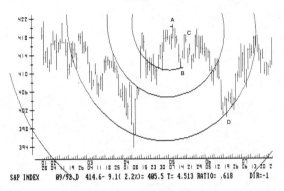

Figure 9–26 Daily S&P chart from 01-92 to 07-92. Spiral turns clockwise, center at point A, starting point at point B, price target at point D. (*Source:* Robert Fischer Research, Chicago.)

On the weekly soybean chart (Figure 9–27) there is another 3-swing pattern given by points *A*, *B*, and *C*. The center of the spiral is at point *A*. The starting point is *B*. The spiral turns counterclockwise. The trend changed when the soybean price penetrated the second ring

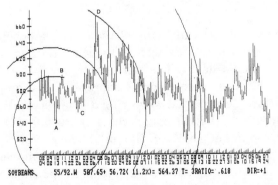

Figure 9–27 Weekly soybean chart from 07-89 to 07-92. Spiral turns counterclockwise, center at point A, starting point at point B, price target at point D. (*Source:* Robert Fischer Research, Chicago.)

of the spiral at point *D*. A short position was entered when the previous 2-week low was broken.

The weekly Treasury bond chart (Figure 9–28) indicates a 3-swing pattern at points *A*, *B*, and *C*. The center of the spiral is at *B*. The starting point is *C*. The spiral turns clockwise. The direction of the trend changed when ring 2 of the spiral was penetrated at point *D*. A short position is entered when the previous 2-week low is broken.

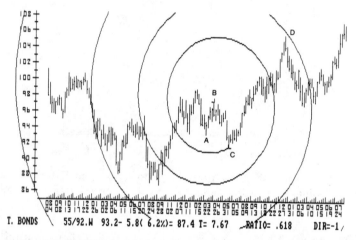

Figure 9–28 Weekly TSY bond chart from 07-89 to 07-92. Spiral turns clockwise, center at point B, starting point at point C, price target at point D. (*Source:* Robert Fischer Research, Chicago.)

Spiral Ring 3

It is not often that the third ring of the spiral is penetrated in the same direction as the major trend. But when it happens a significant trend change should follow. The same entry and exit rules are used that have already been described in Chapter 6. Two examples follow to show what might be expected when ring 3 is penetrated.

On the weekly British pound chart (Figure 9–29) the 3-swing pattern is given by the points *A*, *B*, and *C*. The center of the spiral is at *A*. The starting point is *B*. The spiral turns counterclockwise. The trend changed when the British pound price penetrated ring 3 at point *D*. A short position was set when the valley of the *a-b-c* formation was broken at point *E*.

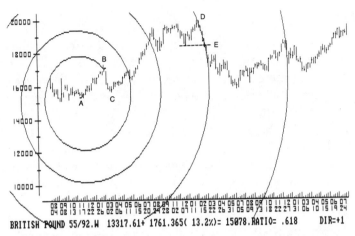

Figure 9-29   Weekly British pound chart from 07-89 to 07-92. Spiral turns counterclockwise, center at point A, starting point at point B, price target at point D.
(*Source:* Robert Fischer Research, Chicago.)

The daily S&P 500 chart (Figure 9–30) gives a 3-swing pattern
at *A*, *B*, and *C*. The center of the spiral is *B*. The starting point is *A*.
The spiral turns counterclockwise. The trend changed when the price
penetrated ring 3 at *D*. A short position was set when the low of the
a-b-c formation is broken at point *E*.

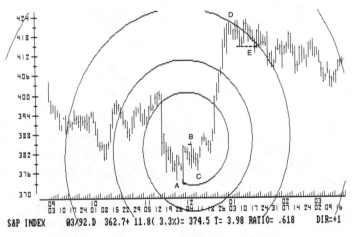

Figure 9-30   Daily S&P chart from 09-91 to 03-92. Spiral turns counterclockwise, center at point B, starting point at point A, price target at point D.
(*Source:* Robert Fischer Research, Chicago.)

Spiral Ring 4

A penetration of ring 4 in the continuing trend direction must occur even less often than any other ring penetration. But it does happen, and should indicate a dramatic trend change. These are moves such as the stock market collapse of October 1987, or extremely long currency trends. They are the ultimate price targets. When ring 4 is penetrated, the point of penetration can be used as an entry signal. There is no need to wait for a confirmation. The stop loss for the currencies should be 100 basis points. The reentry rule, and use of a trailing stop are the same as described in Chapter 6. Two examples follow, using daily and weekly charts, showing the trend changes when ring 4 is penetrated.

The weekly S&P 500 chart shows the 3-swing pattern at A, B, and C (see Figure 9–31). The center of the spiral is B. The starting point is C. The spiral turns counterclockwise. The trend changed when ring 4 of the spiral was broken at point D. A long position can be entered at D, and a stop loss of 400 points placed concurrently.

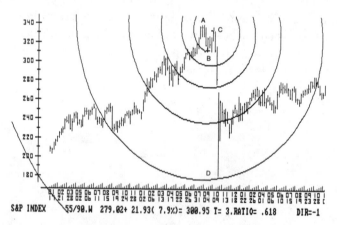

S&P INDEX   55/90.W 279.02+ 21.93(7.9%)= 300.95 T= 3.RATIO= .618   DIR=-1

Figure 9–31   Weekly S&P chart from 01-86 to 10-88. Spiral turns counterclockwise, center at point B, starting point at point C, price target at point D. (*Source:* Robert Fischer Research, Chicago.)

The daily Swiss franc chart (Figure 9–32) has a 3-swing at A, B, and C. The center of the spiral is B. The starting point is A. The spiral turns counterclockwise. The major trend changed when ring 4 was penetrated at D. A long position was set at D along with a stop loss of 100 points.

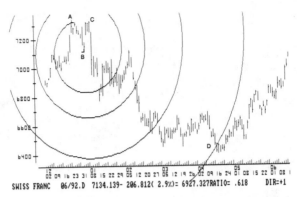

SWISS FRANC   06/92.D 7134.139- 206.812(2.9%)= 6927.327RATIO= .618   DIR=+1

Figure 9–32   Daily Swiss franc chart from 12-91 to 06-92. Spiral turns counter-clockwise, center at point B, starting point at point A, price target at point D. (*Source:* Robert Fischer Research, Chicago.)

Integration of Weekly and Daily Spirals

The spiral analysis should increase in reliability when turning points occur at the same place using different spirals. To show the power of the spiral, Figure 9–33 uses two different Swiss franc time frames to identify the same turning point by applying two different centers and starting points on the weekly chart, and two different centers and starting points on the daily chart.

In all four cases the major turning point *E* could have been identified. This is shown in Figures 9–33a, b, c, and d.

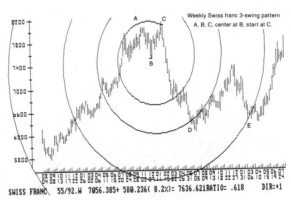

SWISS FRANC   55/92.W 7056.385+ 580.236(8.2%)= 7636.621RATIO= .618   DIR=+1

Figure 9–33a   Weekly Swiss franc chart from 07-89 to 07-92. Spiral turns counterclockwise, center at point B, starting point at point C, price target at point E. (*Source:* Robert Fischer Research, Chicago.)

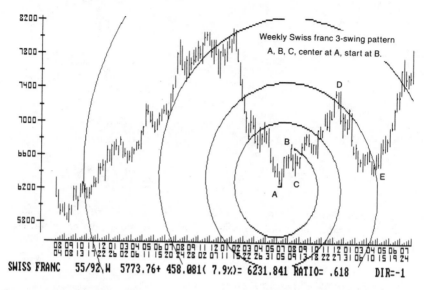

Figure 9–33b   Weekly Swiss franc chart from 07-89 to 07-92. Spiral turns clockwise, center at point A, starting point at point B, price target at point E. (*Source:* Robert Fischer Research, Chicago.)

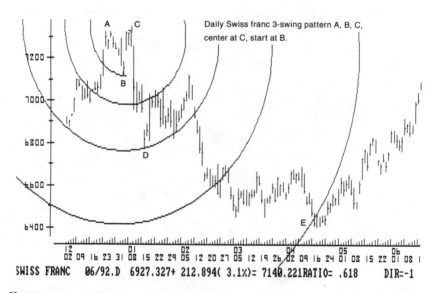

Figure 9–33c   Daily Swiss franc chart from 12-91 to 06-92. Spiral turns counterclockwise, center at point C, starting point at point B, price target at point E. (*Source:* Robert Fischer Research, Chicago.)

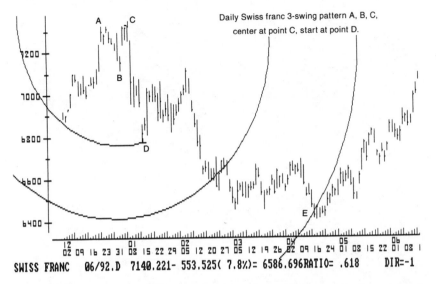

Daily Swiss franc 3-swing pattern A, B, C,
center at point C, start at point D.

SWISS FRANC   06/92.D 7140.221- 553.525(7.8%)= 6586.696RATIO= .618   DIR=-1

Figure 9–33d   Daily Swiss franc chart from 12-91 to 06-92. Spiral turns clockwise, center at point C, starting point at point D, price target at point E. (*Source:* Robert Fischer Research, Chicago.)

SUMMARY

The logarithmic spiral is the link between the Fibonacci summation series and the world of Nature. It is the only mathematical form that expresses the growth pattern seen in the nautilus shell.

Using a computer program to produce the logarithmic spiral, we can find a stunning symmetry in any weekly or daily chart. The secret is to find the center of the spiral. Once this is done, it becomes very likely that turning points in the market can be forecasted accurately.

This forecasting ability is based on the rule of alternation. Elliott discovered this phenomenon and integrated it into his concept. The spiral is the perfect tool to prove the importance of this rule.

This work is only the beginning of a new wave of price analysis; yet, the results of our limited research are too reliable to be accidental. We are able to select eight possibilities which pinpoint every important high and low in the hundreds of charts analyzed. The best overall results can be found using only four of the options.

The spiral provides the solution to the most significant problem in today's price analysis: the integration of time. It is the most logical and promising start.

Appendix A

THE GOLDEN
SECTION COMPASS

The *Golden Section Compass* was introduced at seminars given by the author in 1983. It is an indispensable tool for every investor with an interest in Fibonacci. It is also very easy to use.

The Golden Section Compass is the translation of the Fibonacci summation series into an investment tool. As with a calliper, its points can be drawn closer together or opened wider (Figure A–1). Its three legs always remain separated according to the Fibonacci ratio, thus a dynamic adaption to the cycles is always possible. This is the tool to apply the ratios 0.618 and 1.618 to any chart analysis introduced in this book, with the exception of the spiral (which needs to be generated on a computer). It will help with:

- Corrections,

- Extensions, and

- Time analysis.

Please write to Robert Fischer, 555 W. Madison St., Tower #1, Ste. 1612, Chicago, IL 60661, if you have an interest in acquiring a Golden Section Compass.

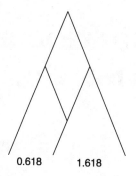

Figure A–1   Golden section compass.

Appendix **B**

SPIRAL EQUATION AND COMPUTER PROGRAM

After the seminars, the Logarithmic Spiral was fully computerized. For investors who are interested in the equation, the following formulas give the necessary details:

Basic Spiral Equation

$$r = ae^{\theta \cot \alpha}$$

For two radii

$$\frac{r_2}{r_1} = \frac{ae^{\theta 2 \cot \alpha}}{ae^{\theta 1 \cot \alpha}} = e^{(\theta 2 - \theta 1)\cot \alpha}$$

For a golden spiral, r_1 and r_2 would be in the ratio

$$\frac{r_2}{r_1} = \phi$$

When r_1 and r_2 are separated by

$$\frac{\pi}{2}$$

Where

$$\phi = \frac{\sqrt{5} + 1}{2}$$

From the above relations, we have

$$\phi - \frac{r_2}{r_1} = e$$

which gives

$$\cot \alpha = \frac{2}{\pi}\, e_n \phi$$

For investors who want to computerize the spiral, the following segment out of our computer program will make it easy to work.

Plot CCW Log Spiral Subroutine

```
13280   '
13290   '
13300   'SPIRAL

        'calculate constant CON using natural log and PHI = (sqrt(5)+1)/2
        'and PI = 3.141593
13320   CON = 2*LOG(1/PHI)/PI

        'find distance RO between center point (P1X, P1Y) and
        'starting point (P2X, P2Y) on spiral
13370   DX = P2X − P1X
13380   DY = P2Y − P1Y
13390   RO = SQR(DX*DX + DY*DY)
13391   IF RO = 0 THEN RETURN

        'find starting angle AO that places RO in the correct quadrant
13392   IF DX < > 0 GOTO 13400
13394   IF DY < 0 THEN AO = −PI/2
13396   IF DY > 0 THEN AO = PI/2
13398   GOTO 13420
13400   AO = ATN(DY/DX)
13410   IF DX < 0 THEN AO = AO + PI

        'A is the angle that will get incremented for each new point
        'by an increment SPINC (=.05, for example) until RMAX is reached
        '(the largest spiral radius you want to calculate)
        'Little short lines are drawn between points (TP1X, TP1Y) and
        '(TP2X, TP2Y) to form the spiral.
        'DIR is = −1 or +1 depending on whether you want a clockwise
        'spiral or a counterclockwise spiral.
13420   A = 0
13430   TP1X = P2X : TP1Y = P2Y

        'loop to calculate and plot each little line segment on the spiral
13440   A = A + SPINC
13450   R = RO*EXP(CON*A)
13460   IF R > RMAX THEN RETURN
13470   TA = A*DIR + AO
13480   TP2X = R*COS(TA) + P1X : TP2Y = R*SIN(TA) + P1Y
13490   LINE (TP1X, TP1Y) − (TP2X, TP2Y)
13500   TP1X = TP2X : TP1Y = TP2Y
13510   GOTO 13440
```

Investors who are interested in our software package should contact Robert Fischer, 555 W. Madison Dr., Tower #1, Suite 1612, Chicago, IL 60661.

INDEX